Catholics at a Crossroads

Also by Eileen P. Flynn

Why Believe? Foundations of Catholic Theology

Issues in Health Care Ethics

Issues in Medical Ethics

Catholicism: Agenda for Renewal

Your Living Will: Why, When and How to Write One

Cradled in Human Hands: A Textbook on Environmental Responsibility

Hard Decisions: Forgoing and Withdrawing Artificial Nutrition and Hydration

Living Faith: An Introduction to Theology

Teaching About AIDS

AIDS: A Catholic Call to Compassion

My Country Right or Wrong? Selective Conscientious Objection in the Nuclear Age

Human Fertilization in Vitro: A Catholic Moral Perspective

Catholics at a Crossroads

Coverup, Crisis, and Cure

by EILEEN P. FLYNN, Ph.D.

PARAVIEW PRESS

NEW YORK

Cover design by Shirley Harryman
Book design by smythtype
ISBN: 1931044465
Library of Congress Catalog Number: 2003100891

To Peggy Greenwood,
thanks for everything.

Contents

Stop

Shall I start with the cabin in the Blue Hills? —where he kept me on my knees all night after servicing him in ways that would make you vomit, if I told you? And how, when he was finished with me he told me that I could now call him Paul, I didn't have to say "Father Shanley" anymore? Or should I move right along to the ruined house in Vermont where in a rage, he left me, without heat or food for an entire day, in the dead of winter, in the middle of nowhere, to teach me that I must never, ever say No to him when he wanted to use me sexually? Or shall I just start first with the dreams that still wake me in sobbing terror and sick to my stomach?

—Arthur Austin[1]

Introduction

Few people are happy with the Catholic Church today. Priests, bishops, cardinals and the pope may seem tranquil on the outside, but they are crying on the inside. Progressives are unhappy about the way the reform-minded agenda of Vatican II has gotten sidetracked, and conservatives bemoan the disintegration of what once was a proud, enviable institution. Collectively, all Catholics suffer from shame and the pain of watching the church lose its credibility and sense of purpose. In the United States concern extends beyond the Catholic community to the broader society. Anticipating his visit with Pope John Paul II on May 29, 2002, President George Bush said that he was distressed and that he needed to share his feelings with the pope: "I will tell him that I am concerned about the Catholic Church in America. I'm concerned about its standing. And I say that because the Catholic Church is an incredibly important institution in our country."[2]

Due primarily to disclosures in 2002 about sexual

molestation cases and the hierarchy's handling of these cases, the Catholic Church is in an alarming decline. Facing what is wrong with the church will be an unnerving experience, but the issue must be confronted. People need to know what is wrong in order to become motivated to correct egregious misconduct. Now is the time to stop and determine the nature of the problems the church is embroiled in so that we can make an accurate assessment and begin to consider corrective measures. Just as youngsters at dangerous intersections are instructed to stop, look, and listen, so we who are at a momentous crossroads in Catholic Church history need to heed these rules. First, we stop to take a serious look at the crisis in the church today.

Statistics on priest molestation

Stating how many priests have sexually molested minors is critically important, but accessing accurate statistics is impossible. There are two reasons for this. The first is that many assaults are never reported and, therefore, never documented. The second is that there is no central data agency that keeps statistics on molestation of minors by priests. Even people who make every effort to gather information are stymied in their quest. Margaret O'Brien Steinfels, editor of the Catholic magazine *Commonweal*, illustrates this fact. When she addressed the Catholic bishops of the United States in Dallas in

June 2002, Mrs. Steinfels said:

> The truth is that we don't know the truth, the
> full truth, about this sex abuse scandal.
> Despite the endless reports ... we don't know
> the truth. Yes, we know some truths—and
> they are horrifying and overwhelming. So
> overwhelming that we can scarcely keep
> track of times and places and numbers. But
> these facts we do know leave many questions
> unanswered...[3]

The estimate that is usually given on the number of
priests who have sexually abused children and adolescents
is approximately two percent. In reviewing a very thorough research study of the files of men who were priests
in Chicago between 1951 and 1991 Philip Jenkins, a
professor at Penn State, wrote that the files showed that
fifty-seven diocesan priests and two visiting priests had
been the subject of allegations of sexual abuse. This
works out to 2.6 percent of that archdiocese's priests having complaints made about their conduct. In 1.7 percent
of cases the charges seemed justified.[4] Citing information
made available by two archdioceses in 2002, Father
Stephen J. Rossetti, a psychologist and the president of
a treatment center for priest sex molesters, agreed that
the number of priests who have molested children and

adolescents is about two percent. Rossetti relied on the archdiocese of Boston's review of its records in 2002, which found "the number of allegations was approximately 60, and it is important to note that this number represents the total number of accused priests over 50 years, ...so the ratio is about 2 percent."[5]

A similar review conducted by the archdiocese of Philadelphia revealed that from 1950 until 2002, 2,154 priests had served and there were "credible allegations" against thirty-five. This is approximately 1.6 percent.[6] From January until June 2002 the number of priests who were forced to leave active ministry because people came forward to accuse them of sexual molestation or because their prior history made them unacceptable risks was 250. "Bishop Wilton D. Gregory, the president of the bishops' conference, responding in Dallas to a request for an estimate of the number of priests facing sanctions, said that about 250 of the nation's 46,000 priests had been suspended from ministry this year."[7] An Associated Press report in December 2002 put the total number of priests who resigned or were removed from duty during the year at 325.[8] Both figures represent less than one percent.

Culture of the Catholic Church
The Catholic Church is an institution and every institution has a culture. The "culture of an institution" refers

to those characteristics that define it and contribute to assumptions about what it is and how it carries on its mission. People make decisions based on implicit understandings about institutions. For example, we know that we should comport ourselves in a dignified manner in a courtroom but we are much less concerned about our behavior at amusement parks. This is because we know that the culture of the court is serious and somber and requires decorum while the culture of an amusement park is relaxed and jovial. What we know has become a perception and we act based on perceptions and assumptions.

The Catholic Church is a complex international institution with a 2,000-year tradition. Hence, commenting on its culture is not a simple matter. Nevertheless, it is possible to consider eight ingrained aspects of the church's culture, all negative, that have given rise to the current crisis involving the priest molestation of minors. The church is supposed to do Christ's work in the world and be a witness to Jesus. If the Catholic Church carried out this mission, it would appear to be a holy institution and people would see it as doing Jesus' work. But, today, people perceive Catholicism as corrupt; the church does not seem to be involved with doing God's work. It is more like a holy mess and a wholehearted campaign to recover its credibility is necessary to restore its image.

1. Hierarchical structure impedes decisive action.

The church is arranged in hierarchical fashion. The Catholic Church is not a democracy. It is a mammoth international institution with more than a billion members, of which approximately 66 million are in the United States, and jurisdiction proceeds from the top down. The pope and his staff at the Vatican set policy and preside at the apex of the organizational pyramid. The pope appoints his assistants (bishops); they carry out his policies and implement them within their jurisdictions (dioceses). Members of the hierarchy profess loyalty to the pope and they invest a great deal of energy in maintaining this loyalty. The way they lead is by looking over their shoulders to determine whether or not the pope is pleased with how they are carrying out their administrative responsibilities and insuring that Catholic doctrine is presented correctly within their dioceses. Accordingly, they are not focused on the requirements of the people under them, not to mention the children of parishioners. It is not that bishops do not care about the people that they lead, only that the system is not set up with the interests of the laity as a primary concern.

Members of the hierarchy should work together to lead the church and serve its members. They should be collaborators and discuss common concerns with the intention of determining how to resolve them. Instead, they act autonomously within their jurisdictions and report only to Rome. Had the United States hierarchy implemented a collaborative element in their ministry they might have come to a communal understanding of the dreadful wrong constituted by priest sexual abuse and might have figured out a common procedure for righting this wrong. They might also have instituted procedures to warn one another about seminarians or priests who were dismissed from their jurisdictions because of sexual abuse of minors. In other words, with a collaborative element, it is more likely that necessary precautions would have been put in place and acted on.

2. Laity exercises a passive role.

Church members are known as laity. Vatican Council II called for the active involvement of lay people in the church.

> Let the spiritual shepherds recognize and promote the dignity as well as the responsibility of the laity in the Church. Let them willingly employ their prudent advice. Let them confidently assign duties to them in the service of the Church, allowing them freedom and room for action. Further, let them encourage lay people so that they may undertake tasks on their own initiative. …(Bishops aided by) the

experience of the laity, can more clearly and more incisively come to decisions regarding both spiritual and temporal matters.[9]

In spite of the Council's mandate to bishops, to a large degree women and men think that all they are expected or allowed to do is to pray, pay and obey. The facts that the laity exercises only a passive role and that men and women docilely accept this role are two negative aspects of Catholic culture that figure in present problems. Lay people have little interaction with members of the hierarchy and there is not much interaction between parishioners and priests at the parish level.

It is lay people, however, who have brought accusations of priest molestation of minors to their pastors or bishops. Why haven't abusive priests been removed after the first credible accusation of misconduct? Why have lay people allowed molester-priests to continue to function in parishes? Simply because the laity has been kept in the dark by both pastors and bishops who consistently tried to conceal the existence of clerical sex abuse. And the laity had no way of learning what was going on.

Following an unprecedented two day summit of American cardinals with the pope and members of the curia in April 2002, a news conference was held at which Cardinal Theodore Mc Carrick of Washington, D. C., was asked why the statement that was issued had no reference to how lay Catholics were going to assist in resolving the crisis. Mc Carrick answered, "Words were in. Words were out," of the hastily prepared statement and even though lay people were not specifically referred to in the document, there would be an important role for them to play.[10] What role? What would it consist of? How critical would it be? By not addressing these questions from the outset, the top Catholic leadership continues to give the impression that the laity plays a passive role in the church.

3. Priests are considered superior.

Priests make vows of celibacy by which they promise to sacrifice sexual gratification in marriage in order to be fully available to serve Catholic people. In the sacramental tradition of the church the priest represents Christ. It is a priest who presides at the Eucharist, pronouncing the sacred words of consecration over the bread and wine. "This is my body; this is my blood." The church believes him to be an *alter Christus,* another Christ, as he says mass and administers the sacrament of Penance. During the rite of Penance the priest proclaims "I forgive you your sins in the name of the Father, and of the Son, and of the Holy Spirit." The belief of the church is that Jesus uses his representative, a priest, to bring about reconciliation between God and sinners.

How can it be that some of the same priests who are

held in such exalted regard have transgressed boundaries and molested children? One reason is that priests have been placed on pedestals and revered based on their religious functioning without thinking that they too can act as criminals who break laws.

In an account that details a session during which one hundred men from Kentucky spoke about being molested years after the abuse occurred, the notion that it was unthinkable that a priest should do such a thing was articulated by a victim, Mike Turner. "For you to go up and tell anybody that a priest did something to you, you might as well say God did it to you," he said. Another victim, Dr. Boswell Tabler, fifty-two, who was assaulted when he was in parochial school, concurred. "That is absolutely correct," he said. "We are taught the priest is God's representative on earth."[11] From this example we can understand that the holiness and superior status that people automatically assign to priests prevent children from telling their parents about what happened to them and keep parents from even imagining the possibility that such misconduct could occur.

4. Confusion over celibacy and sexuality of priests

Based on the fact that priests commit themselves to celibacy people have wrongly concluded that priests are nonsexual and that this aspect of their personalities has been shut down so that they do not have sexual needs and do not experience sexual urges. Because of their commitment to serve their parishes, priests tend to be revered and people tend to think that priests will be excellent influences on their children. Hence, parents are happy if their child has an association with a priest. The underlying hope of parents is that this association will be a means to counteract bad influences that are rampant in society, such as drugs and promiscuity.

Just as Catholic people expect priests to be nonsexual, so priest-molesters have never gotten to a stage of development in which they understand their aberrant desires. Trained in a seminary culture that did not address sexual paraphilias, priest-offenders do not know that they should deal with their problem by consulting mental health professionals. Furthermore, not knowing that pedophilia, which entails sex between an adult man and a prepubescent child, and ephebophilia, which entails sex between an adult man and an adolescent minor, are psychiatric disorders hampers predator priests from taking steps to deal with these terrible dysfunctions. Since they live in a world that does not address what preoccupies them, priest-molesters cope by bifurcating themselves; there exist simultaneously the dutiful priest who performs his sacred functions and the molester who attacks children or adolescents. Priest offenders manage to function by acknowledging the existence of the former while denying the existence of the latter.

5. Children are not capable of acting in their own best interest.

In the past, most children who were molested by priests thought that it might have been their fault. Confused and traumatized at the outset, they are also likely to have believed that the sexual actions must be acceptable because the priest initiated them and he is above reproach. Often youngsters are too ashamed or embarrassed to tell their parents, or they are afraid of the priest's retaliation if they do. Frequently, too, the priest-molester's admonition "not to tell" keeps them quiet, as does the conviction that no one would believe them.

6. Parents were dismissed when they contacted authorities.

Up until recently, if parents found out what happened to their child, they were likely to confront a pastor or bishop with the story. Given the culture of the church, however, until the Gauthe case in 1985, disclosure of abuse was not likely to result in removal of a priest from contact with children. Pastors and bishops unfailingly promised parents and guardians that they would take care of everything and that the problem Father would not be reassigned to a parish unless appropriate authorities cleared him. Parents tended to take bishops at their word; they would have considered themselves bad Catholics had they not done so.

7. Priest shortage resulted in reassignments.

In view of the kinds of reassurances that pastors and bishops were wont to give, why have there been so many incidents of priests reassigned to parishes where they found more victims and committed crimes against more children? The answer lies in how the church has operated. Two aspects of church structure resulted in transfers. First, bishops are responsible for staffing parishes and other Catholic facilities. For the past thirty years there has been an ever-worsening priest shortage so that the census of priests is always less than last year and the ratio of priests to parishioners is in constant decline. By the year 2005, according to Robert Schoenherr and Lawrence A. Young in *Full Pews and Empty Altars* (1993), there will be 21,000 active diocesan priests, down from 35,000 in 1966. Almost half will be fifty-five or older. They think that the decline in priestly ordinations is a more significant cause of the shortage than resignation and retirement of older priests.

This situation put bishops at a distinct disadvantage. Because they did not have anyone else to fill positions, bishops took a chance and reassigned priest-molesters who had been treated by counselors. As a matter of fact, as recently as March, 2002, the priest shortage in northern Maine led Bishop Joseph J. Gerry to ask parish councils whether they wanted to retain two pastors who each admitted to a single case of sex abuse involving adolescent boys many years before.[12] From the outset Bishop Gerry said that whatever the votes, he alone would make the final decisions. A reason he wanted parish councils to consider keeping their pastors is germane: "Few places have been affected more by the priest shortage than this remote community a few miles south of the Canadian border. Four churches have closed in the past five years."[13] Both bishop and parishioners faced the same grim eventuality: If these pastors were removed, there might be no other priests available to take their place. And, if a replacement were found, it was unlikely that he would share the cultural heritage of the French Canadian Catholics in St. John Valley. (On March 10, 2002, Bishop Gerry announced that he had decided to remove the priests in question after "a new accusation of sexual misconduct against one of them surfaced this (past) week, and because of what he called 'the recent events in Boston.'"[14]

Second, bishops and priests are brothers in a tight fraternity and bishops rely on priests to do the work of the church. In order to lessen the likelihood of priest demoralization, bishops gave abusers the benefit of the doubt and allowed them to resume ministry after completion of counseling programs. They stood by their priests. Bishops thought that by doing this all priests under their jurisdiction would think that their bishops were on their side and this would motivate feelings of loyalty. Bishops considered this state of affairs advantageous for the church; they did not foresee how such a purported advantage would lead to the worst imaginable situation for the institution they govern.

8. Bishops exercise considerable monetary discretion.

The Catholic Church is structured in dioceses, geographic areas presided over by bishops. The bishop has great leeway in the way he administers his diocese. Diocesan funds come from parishes that make up the diocese. Each parish is assessed a percentage of its weekly collections and must turn that money over to the bishop. In addition, bishops can raise more money by instituting annual appeals that assess parishes' specific amounts; campaigns are conducted to raise these assessments. The end result of the ability of bishops to raise funds is that bishops wind up with significant amounts of money at their disposal. Since lay people play a passive role and since priests know better than to ask for an accounting of expenditures, the culture of the church has allowed bishops access to money to use at their discretion. In regard to sexual abuse claims that come from victims represented by lawyers, bishops have been able to allot financial settlements on the condition that accusers agree to abide by confidentiality agreements. These agreements are meant to insure that the good name of the church is not besmirched by details of the crimes of priest molesters. What bishops, their lawyers and accountants did not anticipate was that the façade of silence that was skillfully crafted throughout the United States over a period of almost twenty years would disintegrate in Boston in 2002 and from then on they would need a totally new approach to public relations.

A settlement paid by former Milwaukee Archbishop Rembert Weakland to Paul J. Marcoux illustrates the hierarchy's control over money. When Marcoux was thirty-three years old he had an encounter with Weakland that Marcoux characterized as "date rape."[15] Twenty years later Weakland, pressured by Marcoux, executed a confidential financial settlement with him for $450,000. The archbishop did not deny that he had a sexual relationship with Marcoux but did implicitly deny the characterization by Marcoux of the nature of their intimacy by saying, "I have never abused anyone."[16]

Revelations about the payment left Milwaukee Catholics profoundly uneasy and had them asking who was involved in authorizing such a large payment. The answer from spokesperson Jerry Topczewski was that "Nothing was done out of the ordinary in processing this settlement" and that along with Archbishop Weakland, three other people knew of the settlement: the archdiocese's lawyer, its auxiliary bishop and its finance officer.[17] Thus, the only likely way that word of the payoff would get out was if the victim broke his agreement and spoke up. The archbishop and those who worked for him could be counted on to keep silence and the archbishop had the power to write a check for almost half a million dollars to keep his sexual dalliance from public knowledge.

Rejection of standard excuses

Nowadays people are reluctant to accept the standard excuse that, in the past, church leadership did their best to protect children considering the limited extent of knowledge then available, but, today, given greater understanding, bishops promise that actions will be different and children will not be endangered. This excuse does not ring true because of the abdication of responsibility that it allows in respect to bishops' past accountability. Frequently bishops bolster their position with the claim that they are bishops and, as such, do not enjoy competence as evaluators of human behavior. They correctly state that understanding human behavior is the province of psychiatrists and psychologists and they explain that in the past they relied on the advice of these professionals in reassigning priest-offenders. In other words, they were guided by reports that said that a given priest had completed a program of therapy and did not seem to pose a threat to children. What bishops fail to address is that most normal, intelligent people balk at reassigning a multiple abuser who had committed abuse in more than one parish. They would see repeated instances of abuse as a signal to exercise caution and not put children in harm's way.

The bishops' bureaucratic defense does not stand up against the "reasonable person standard." According to this standard, sane, reasonable people would not take one chance, let alone several chances, by placing priests who had molested children in proximity to more children. Concern for vulnerable children would be paramount. The need to staff parishes, while an important administrative responsibility, would not take precedence over the requirement that those in authority keep innocent children from harm. That so many Catholic bishops failed to safeguard children exposes their timidity and lack of moral integrity. Just as it is hard to get a precise accounting of how many priests molested children, so it is difficult to come up with an accurate count of how many bishops did not act decisively to prevent abusive priests from continuing their ministry. In light of the fact that dioceses across the United States are now facing litigation involving priest molestation, it is fair to surmise that the negligence of bishops has been widespread. Information provided on June 12, 2002, by Dallas News online, following a three-month investigation, supports this assertion:

> Roughly two-thirds of top U.S. Catholic leaders have allowed priests accused of sexual abuse to keep working, a systematic practice that spans decades and continues today, a three-month *Dallas Morning News* review shows. The study—the first of its kind—looked at the records of the top leaders of the nation's 178 mainstream Roman Catholic dioceses, including acting administrators in cases where the top job is vacant.[18]

Manuals of moral theology that bishops studied when they were in seminaries instructed them that in instances of doubt one should follow the safer course. The example of a hunter in the woods who was unsure whether the object in the distance was a human or a deer was used to illustrate that the hunter was ethically required not to shoot because he might kill a person. Human reason required that the hunter follow the safer course. Like the hunter, we can expect that a bishop should have enough common sense not to reassign a repeat molester because the priest might well do it again.

Peter Steinfels, a *New York Times* religion correspondent, correctly states that there were two significant breakthroughs in understanding the nature of priest sex abuse of minors. These benchmark events had a significant impact on how bishops comprehended the nature of the problem. The first event happened in 1985 when the case of Father Gilbert Gauthe played out in Louisiana. Gauthe molested dozens of boys and sensational coverage of his case led to awareness that "sexual molestation was a deep-seated compulsion, demanding treatment and possibly removal from the priesthood."[19]

If bishops did not stop and acknowledge lessons learned from the Gauthe episode, the far more sensational case that occurred eight years later got their attention. "In 1993, the trial and conviction of James Porter, a former priest in Fall River, Mass., … drove these lessons home to many bishops."[20] Porter molested more than two hundred children in five states. Based on the information generated by the Gauthe and Porter cases, when the question, "What did the bishops know, and when did they know it?" is raised, less blame can be laid at their feet prior to 1985 than afterwards. As of 1993, it is fair to say that bishops had no legitimate excuse for saying that they were ignorant about the nature of sexual paraphilias. From that time forward it made sense to expect decisive action from them in removing predatory priests from ministry. That action was not forthcoming.

Don't blame the messenger

Bishops need to stop trying to turn the tables on their critics and accusing them of bashing the Catholic Church. It is dishonest to say, "The church is fine but the bigots or sensationalists who do not like us want to discredit us." People will not be misled by this explanation. The media and the lawyers are not the problem; the media and the lawyers have brought the church's problems to light and we need to acknowledge this. Church hierarchy will not begin to recover credibility until bishops acknowledge that they have been egregiously negligent and they are willing to take appropriate action.

New Jersey talk show host and newspaper columnist Steve Adubato writes that some in the church acknowledge the severity of the problem and the responsibility that must be taken. One of those is Camden, New Jersey, Bishop Nicholas DiMarzio who clearly states what should be obvious to everyone, "We cannot blame the situation on the media, overzealous attorneys, or those who would seek somehow to undermine the church…It must be made unmistakably clear that sexual abuse by clergy is a grave wrong and can never be tolerated."[21]

Prejudiced attacks against Catholics were common when Catholics were largely uneducated immigrants. There were few Catholics in those days with the self-confidence and media savvy to expose biased, ignorant statements for what they were. In the half century since World War II, however, Catholics in the United States have come of age. Catholics make up the largest religious group in the nation and their bishops have media consultants. This is not to say that a prejudiced attack against Catholics would be impossible, only that it would quickly be dismissed for what it is.

Since the 1980s the church has invested a great deal of money in maintaining its public relations image. Estimates on the amount spent on sex abuse settlements range from hundreds of millions to one billion dollars.[22] Roderick MacLeish, Jr., a Boston attorney who has represented more than one hundred victims, estimates that the expense of dealing with victims will be a multibillion-dollar problem for the church before it is over.[23] Exposed to a harsh media spotlight since the beginning of 2002, members of the hierarchy have resorted, in desperation, to attacking members of the media for portraying the church in a bad light by running with, exaggerating, and sensationalizing the sex abuse story. The church should acknowledge how horrendous the truth reported by the media is and stop portraying itself as a victim. Blaming any group is uncalled for. In the past, blaming communists, socialists, capitalists, liberals, narcissists, Protestants, feminists, secularists or sensationalists for the problems of the Catholic Church was a familiar tactic but, at the present time, this strategy is totally inefficient. Abused children and their loved ones are the sole victims and this fact should be kept clearly in view.

The year the truth emerges

On January 10, 2002, less than a week before the beginning of a civil trial against Father John Geoghan who was accused of sexual abuse of more than 130 children, during a span of thirty years in several parishes and convicted of fondling one boy, Cardinal Bernard Law apologized. "With all my heart I wish to apologize for the harm done to the victims of sexual abuse by priests," Law said, appearing, according to a journalist, humbled without the mitre and vestments that are traditional parts of a cardinal's attire. "I am indeed profoundly sorry."[24] In view of the aftermath of the cases against Gilbert Gauthe (1985) and James Porter (1993) both Cardinal Law and members of the public at large probably thought that the reach of Geoghan's case would be limited to that priest and his victims and that the church would carry on much as it had after other big cases. However, this familiar pattern was breached by extensive, sustained publicity about the vile details of

Geoghan's crimes along with unrelenting reporting of the fact that complaints to the Boston archdiocese about Geoghan were dismissed. Again and again he was reassigned and continued his criminal acts of molestation. The matter of egregious negligence on the part of Geoghan's superiors was joined and the way the hierarchy governs the church saw scrutiny by the media as never before.

As John Geoghan's case made its way through the court in Boston, charges against priests all across the United States followed with astounding frequency. Especially distressing was information that two successive bishops of the diocese of Palm Beach, Florida, had molested minors. After acknowledging wrongdoing, Bishop Keith Symons stepped down in 1998 and Bishop Anthony O'Connell was named to replace him. Bishop O'Connell resigned in 2002 when information surfaced about a settlement he made with Christopher Dixon, a former seminarian, who accused O'Connell of molestation when Dixon was a teenager in a Missouri seminary.[25]

A staccato drumbeat of charges continued to attract attention. Cardinal Edward Egan of New York came under criticism for his handling of priest sex abuse cases while he was bishop of Bridgeport, Connecticut, mostly in regard to reassignment of abusers after treatment. Bishops Robert Banks of Green Bay, Wisconsin,

Thomas Dailey of Brooklyn, John McCormack of Manchester, New Hampshire, and William Murphy of Rockville Center, New York, were criticized for their handling of Fathers Geoghan and Shanley when they held administrative posts in the archdiocese of Boston.[26] In Camden, New Jersey, where a civil trial was under way to establish the rights of victims of priest sex abuse to sue the diocese after expiration of the statute of limitations, the judge hearing the case criticized the diocese for its hard hitting tactics designed to thwart victims.[27] Mark Serrano broke his confidentiality agreement to talk about what he endured at the hands of Father James Hanley, a priest of the Diocese of Paterson, New Jersey. Serrano was enraged that Hanley had been reassigned after the bishop knew of his crimes against Serrano. How could Hanley have been placed in new parishes where he had access to more children?

The bishop of Paterson, Frank Rodimer, met with Serrano and other victims of Father Hanley; at these meetings it was impossible for the bishop to avoid the contempt of Hanley's victims.[28] While talks between Hanley's victims and Rodimer were ongoing, the matter of a $250,000 settlement made by Rodimer based on the fact that he shared a vacation house with another priest, Peter Osinski who was convicted of sexually abusing a boy at that house, came to light. In this regard, Rodimer declared that he would personally repay the diocese the amount of the settlement entered into on his behalf.[29]

Bishop J. Kendrick Williams of Lexington, Kentucky stepped aside on May 23, 2002, after allegations surfaced that he had committed sexual abuse. Bishop Williams denied the accusations, "I am stunned and saddened by this accusation. Let me state this simply: the allegations are false."[30] On June 11, 2002, while still maintaining his innocence, Williams resigned as bishop following accusations from three additional men who accused him of abuse from 1969 to 1981.[31]

On June 12, 2002, Bishop James F. McCarthy who held the position of auxiliary bishop in charge of the northern area of the archdiocese of New York resigned because of "sexual affairs with women over the course of several years." While reports stated that none of the women was a minor and McCarthy's conduct was not illegal, given the tenor of the sex abuse climate, he had to resign as bishop.[32]

In Los Angeles there were disclosures that Cardinal Roger Mahoney allowed Father Michael Stephen Baker to continue to work in parishes after Father Baker disclosed to Mahoney "in 1986 that he had abused some boys."[33] Father Baker was not forced to retire until 2000, and Cardinal Mahoney apologized for his failure not to take firm and decisive action much earlier.

Two priests accused of sex abuse of minors committed suicide in April and May 2002, Father Dan Rooney of Cleveland, Ohio,[34] and Father Alfred J. Bietighofer of Bridgeport, Connecticut.[35] The suicide of Father Bietighofer led to an investigation of the St. Luke Institute in Silver Spring, Maryland, where the priest was being treated. As a result of this investigation, the Joint Commission on Accreditation of Healthcare Organizations charged that there were "serious problems at St. Luke in monitoring patients and screening them for the risk of suicide, dispensing medicine and staffing." Rev. Stephen J. Rossetti, the president of St. Luke, a facility specializing in treating priests with sexual and other serious psychological and addictive problems, said steps would be taken to correct the deficiencies.[36]

In the spring of 2002, Catholic lay people began meeting in Boston to decide on how they could play a positive role in setting the church aright. Despite Cardinal Law's objections to their request to share in decision-making, Voice of the Faithful—a grassroots group that was determined to stand with victims, support good priests, and require structural change in church administration—carried on, convinced of the rightness of their cause.[37] Meanwhile, Catholics in New Hampshire, troubled by the way their bishop, John McCormack, handled priest abusers while he was personnel administrator in Boston, circulated a petition asking that he step down.[38] Some Boston Catholics, more radical than those in Voice of the Faithful, carried on a noisy campaign for Cardinal Bernard Law to resign because they believed he had lost the moral authority to lead the archdiocese.

Media coverage of sex abuse of minors by Catholic clergy became so relentless that Archbishop John J. Myers of Newark thought it necessary to voice an objection. "Of course we applaud the efforts of anyone who wishes to protect children and adults too, for that matter, from any kind of abuse," he said. "And we certainly acknowledge the media's responsibility to report the news. At the same time, one cannot help but wonder if the constant barrage of publicity is directed to that noble end or if it is directed toward increasing circulation or viewership or profits or even intended to lessen the credibility of the consistent teaching of the Church."[39]

Shell shocked by the ferocity of the exposure, like Myers, many Catholics complained about the sheer volume and sensationalistic aspects of the stories. Complaints notwithstanding, publicity continued so that by mid-2002 and thereafter there was near universal agreement that the Catholic Church was in crisis and that radical change was necessary. The status quo had to be abandoned and future governance of the church needed to change to break with former standard operating procedures.

During the 1980's and 1990's when spokespersons

for the church addressed the media about occasional sex abuse cases the typical response was that there is no statistical difference between the incidence of priests who abuse minors and the occurrence of pederasty in the general population. Thus, it is incorrect to think of the priesthood as a profession that attracts or harbors a disproportionate number of pedophiles or ephebophiles. Spokespersons also emphasized the vulnerability of priests who are at risk of being falsely accused. They said that false accusations can easily happen because people can be lured by the hope of receiving monetary settlements, they can be mentally unstable or they can be motivated by personal vendettas. The fact that baseless charges of abuse were brought against the late Cardinal Joseph Bernardin of Chicago in 1993 bolstered this contention. These standard defenses, regularly articulated, bought the Catholic hierarchy more than a decade's grace in keeping sexual abuse by Catholic priests on the periphery of public awareness and keeping themselves from having to stand accountable for reassigning abusers. With the widespread revelations that began in 2002, however, this public relations strategy evaporated.

The new awareness of cases of priest sex abuse of minors as well as reassignments for abuser priests led to a consensus for the need to open this matter to a thorough public airing. People became aware of the inability of the Catholic hierarchy to administer the church with credibility and implement defensible staffing policies. There was no question that priests who sexually molest children are sinners and criminals, but bishops who oversee these offender priests were egregiously negligent and excuses made by them to defend their lapses of judgment were not acceptable. Saying 'sorry' became insufficient.

Even given the context of the disclosures about Father John Geoghan, which triggered media coverage of sexual molestation by priests in the Catholic Church, Father Paul Shanley's case, which arose as the Geoghan case was being resolved in court, is absolutely astounding. Present at the founding meeting for NAMBLA, the North American Man-Boy Love Association, a pro-pedophilia group, Shanley advocated bizarre sexual ideas that were completely at odds with Catholic teaching as well as with the safety of young boys.[40] He actually said that sex between men and boys was acceptable and that the boys looked for and enjoyed it. Evidence in church files shows that officials knew of sexual misconduct allegations against Shanley as early as 1967.[41] In spite of numerous complaints during more than twenty years, Shanley continued to work as a priest in the archdiocese of Boston. Several times he was sent away for counseling and treatment and then reassigned.[42] In 1990 Shanley was placed on sick leave in Boston and he moved to California where he co-owned, with another priest, a motel that catered to a gay clientele, a very strange sideline for a man who was simultaneously exercising priestly ministry.[43] Yet in a letter, Robert J. Banks, then an assistant to Cardinal Law in Boston, and currently bishop in Green Bay, Wisconsin, stated that Shanley should be "of no concern" to the California parish where he worked.[44]

A report in the *Los Angeles Times* highlights events after 1995 when Shanley had left California and moved to New York:

> By 1991, it seems that the evidence was incontrovertible. The archdiocese paid a $40,000 settlement to a man who said Shanley had raped him repeatedly in 1972, when he was 12 or 13. The Rev. John McCormack, a seminary classmate of Shanley's wrote in a memo to Bishop Alfred Hughes, Law's point man for daily archdiocesan operations, "It is clear to me that Paul Shanley is a sick person." But in 1995, Shanley had moved to New York and was working at Leo House, a church guesthouse frequented by student travelers. A 1996 letter from Law to Shanley upon his retirement praises his "impressive record," saying, "You are truly appreciated for all that you have

done." In (a) 1997 letter, Law allows that "…as you know, some controversy for his past has followed him to New York" but says he did not object to Shanley's application to be director of the New York City guesthouse. Another memo to Law, however, indicates that Shanley did not get the top job, not because of any threat to boys and young men but because New York's Cardinal John O'Connor "feels the situation in the Leo House neighborhood is too volatile to risk the publicity which might arise."[45]

In spite of the incredible particulars of Paul Shanley's history, after retiring in 1995, he remained a free man living in an apartment complex in San Diego. No one monitored his comings, goings or guests, or warned parents that he might be a danger to neighborhood children. Paul Shanley's freedom ended in 2002 when he returned to Boston to face criminal charges of sexual molestation.

Based on everything that has become known since January 2002, attention is now focused on the fact that church governance has been extremely negligent in regard to the welfare of children. Keeping the celibacy requirement for the priesthood, which attracts an insufficient number of prospects, together with the bureaucratic management of dioceses that directs attention to carrying out policies emanating from Rome have resulted in dangerous situations. Priest abusers were regularly reassigned and innocent children were put in harm's way. In many ways the complicity of the hierarchy has emerged as more disturbing than the fact that there are priests who are pederasts. The negligence of the hierarchy has become the foremost issue.

With the media coverage in 2002, people throughout the United States learned about legal and financial aspects of the sex abuse crisis. On the legal side were disclosures about how hard-hitting church lawyers are who deal with victims who seek financial settlements. Remarks by Judge John G. Himmelberger, Jr., of Atlantic County Superior Court in New Jersey, illustrate this point. Judge Himmelberger excoriated the decision of the diocese of Camden to vigorously contest the lawsuit of two brothers who wanted the statute of limitations waived so that they could sue for damages many years after they allege that they suffered abuse at the hands of Monsignor Philip Rigney from 1975 until 1983. Although Robert and Philip Young did not sue until the statute of limitations had expired, forcing the judge to reject their request, he said that the abuse they described in his courtroom was "horrific" and left evident emotional scars. Additionally, the judge criticized the Camden diocese for using "hardball" tactics and said,

"The church's position in this litigation is at odds with its stance as a moral force in society."[46]

Another legal issue that has come to light is that of confidentiality agreements entered into between church authorities and sex abuse victims. According to these legal settlements the church agrees to pay an amount of money to a victim to settle any and all claims the person has against the institutional church provided that the victim agrees never to disclose details about the actions that caused harm. Many people who signed these agreements say that they now want the catharsis that might come from talking about what happened to them. They are also angry that priests who molested them were reassigned and they want to strike back at the church. They think it would help them if they could vent their anger and tell their stories. Understandably, the Catholic hierarchy does not want salacious details to come to light but, in this regard, public opinion seems to be turning against the bishops. People who have been dismayed to learn that priest abusers were reassigned without the knowledge of their past crimes disclosed to pastors or parishioners say that the time is right to bring everything into the open and release those who agreed to settlements from confidentiality requirements.

In regard to yielding ground on statutes of limitation, bishops have routinely instructed their attorneys not to enter into deals that would be favorable to plaintiffs.

Specifics of statutes of limitation vary from state to state but, in general, these regulations allow a victim only a set number of years after reaching adulthood to bring charges against a molester. The number of years is counted from the date when the plaintiff reaches sixteen or eighteen and, in most cases, the plaintiff has ten years following that birthday to bring charges. By holding to strict enforcement of statute of limitation rules, bishops lessen the amount that dioceses pay in settlements. Given the nature of the suffering that victims endure and the years it may take before victims become able to talk about what happened to them, public opinion is moving in the direction of siding with those who were abused rather than endorsing strict adherence to statutes.

A previously unimaginable law was passed by the California state legislature in June 2002. It revokes the California statute of limitations on cases of sexual abuse of minors for the one year beginning on January 1, 2003. This means that in California, during 2003, victims may bring charges against molesters regardless of how many years have elapsed since alleged abuse took place. Victim advocates say that, "The new law, which applies only to civil cases, could make California's courts the next major battleground in the priest sexual abuse scandal."[47]

Officials of dioceses in California, fearing for the financial solvency of the church, embarked on a public relations campaign to overturn the law or, at least, to make Catholics think twice about suing the church for something that may have happened (or, as they imply, may *not* have happened) a long time ago. To this end, a letter was read from pulpits on December 8, 2002. It stated: "Some of the lawsuits may involve the revival of already settled cases and some may involve alleged perpetrators and witnesses long since dead. Under those circumstances it will be difficult, if not impossible, to ascertain the truth."[48] While, in the past, it would have been unthinkable that Catholic leaders would be making these types of arguments, in the current climate the new California law is just one among many developments.

Financial disclosures in conjunction with the sex abuse crisis are very unsettling. Insurers who in the past were willing to write policies for the church covering costs associated with claims arising from incidents of priest sex abuse have stopped providing coverage because they are unwilling to tolerate concomitant exposure.[49] Meeting settlement costs without the assistance of insurers may threaten the financial solvency of dioceses that do not have significant reserves. In Boston in May 2002, the archdiocese reneged on a multimillion-dollar settlement agreement with eighty-six victims of John Geoghan because of a decision by the finance council that the archdiocese did not have enough money to pay what Cardinal Law and the victims' lawyers had agreed upon.[50]

By December 2002 the situation in Boston had deteriorated to such a degree that the finance council voted to allow the archdiocese to file for bankruptcy.[51] This vote "does not mean the archdiocese will definitely declare bankruptcy"[52] but it does indicate that church leaders are considering the advantages of such a declaration. (According to church law, a diocese needs Vatican approval before taking a step such as declaring bankruptcy.)

In Boston attorneys who are seeking financial settlements from the church represent more than 450 plaintiffs. Without bankruptcy protection, compensating these people for the sex abuse they allege they experienced at the hands of priests could require payouts of an estimated 100 million dollars or more, a sum that might liquidate the assets of the Catholic Church in Boston.[53] With bankruptcy protection, the court would award a smaller amount and more financial assets could be retained by the archdiocese.

The decision to consider bankruptcy followed a setback for the Boston archdiocese at the hands of Judge Constance M. Sweeney. On November 25, 2002, Judge Sweeney ordered the release of more than 11,000 pages of documents containing accusations of abuse against scores of priests.[54] The archdiocese had tried to prevent release of the material but Judge Sweeney rejected its arguments and said that the church's records "raise significant questions of whether the archdiocese was really exercising the care they claimed to use in assigning offending priests."[55]

With release of the documents the public learned new, prurient details about clergy sexual abuse as well as the fact that as recently as 1996 Cardinal Law had sympathized with "the pain endured by those who have been accused."[56] Despite Law's protestations that he had been decisive in dealing with sex abusers for the past ten years, his own handwriting disclosed his duplicity.

Details about the misconduct of heretofore-unknown priest-molesters triggered new felt alarm. In Weymouth, Massachusetts, Rev. Robert Meffen allegedly recruited girls in the late 1960s to become nuns and then sexually assaulted them.[57] Rev. Thomas Forry allegedly built a house on Cape Cod for a woman with whom he carried on an eleven-year affair. Even though archdiocesan officials knew about Forry, they allowed him to continue to serve as a priest.[58] A third priest, Rev. Richard Buntel provided cocaine to boys as barter for sex.[59]

Given the fact that church files reveal horrific stories that make people angry with Catholic leaders and unsympathetic to them, the current climate is suitable for making the archdiocese of Boston pay a lot of money for the negligence of the cardinal and his assistants.

Bankruptcy, however, would be a two-edged sword, bringing both advantages and disadvantages. On one hand, a bankrupt archdiocese would probably pay out a lot less in settlement damages than if it were operating in the black and bankruptcy is a slow process that would work in the church's favor. Attorneys would be inclined to take modest offers rather than hold out for large cash settlements. Additionally, the Boston archdiocese would get a fresh start with a new judge who might have a different attitude on open proceedings and go easier on it than Judge Sweeney has.[60] Future requirements of less disclosure would benefit Catholic leaders who cannot withstand the scrutiny that follows full disclosure.

On the other hand, however, "bankruptcy would not necessarily mean that the archdiocese would have to pay less to plaintiffs."[61] And declaring bankruptcy would mean that the leader of the Boston archdiocese would give up control over the church's assets to a bankruptcy judge who would have authority over "major financial decisions, such as what land, buildings and other assets the archdiocese might sell."[62] The judge would also have unfettered access to ledgers previously never opened to government officials or other external auditors. This would represent a stunning reversal of stature for the Catholic Church in the United States. Never in its history has a diocese or archdiocese declared bankruptcy and submitted to control by an external authority. So searing is the nature of the scandal that one of the nation's Catholic strongholds has been brought to this precipice. The archdiocese of Boston is likely to teeter on the brink for quite some time before the matter of bankruptcy is resolved.

An unprecedented step was taken when Cardinal Bernard Law, the most powerful member of the hierarchy in the United States, resigned his office in Rome on December 13, 2002.[63] Analysts immediately set out to determine what it was that made Law finally step down. Was it that the Vatican thought that the time had come? Was it because collections and attendance were down at Boston churches? Was it because fifty-eight priests from Boston signed a letter requesting the cardinal's resignation? Had Law just had enough, and more than enough? Or was the reason future oriented? Did Cardinal Law fear what would happen when the just-convened grand jury released its findings? Did he foresee criminal charges against him for conspiracy or aiding and abetting felonies?

We probably will never know what prompted Cardinal Law's resignation. But people do seem to know that Cardinal Law, Vatican officials, and leaders of the American Catholic Church made an enormous miscalculation when they thought that they could keep their critics at arm's length, circle the miters and repeatedly say "I'm sorry." On January 10, 2002, as John Geoghan's trial was set to begin, Cardinal Bernard Law said, "With all my heart I wish to apologize for the harm done to the victims of sexual abuse by priests." He again apologized profusely when he finally resigned. His words then, and throughout 2002, with all that year's horrific news, were totally insufficient. Sorry was not enough. Change is needed, radical structural change that will result in a credible Catholic Church.

Thus, 2002 was a daunting time for the Catholic Church in the United States. None of the news was good, and members of the hierarchy could not deflect horrible publicity. The church was in crisis and crisis can be looked at in two ways, as a time of extreme trouble or as a turning point.

Trauma of victims

Ninety percent of priest sexual misconduct is with boys, and in ninety percent of cases, which involve boys, the boys are thirteen or fourteen to seventeen years old. Regardless of the form of molestation – be it fondling, embracing, exhibitionism, kissing, oral sex performed on the minor or oral sex requested by the priest and performed on him, mutual masturbation or rape with vaginal or anal penetration – the youngster suffers emotional distress. The more painful and penetrating the sexual assaults and the longer the period of time during which sexual abuse goes on, the more extensive the trauma.

There is no one pattern of emotional trauma experienced by all victims of sexual abuse because personal development varies from individual to individual. Nevertheless, commonalities are seen in the lives of people assaulted by priests. Soon after initial episodes of abuse, children may appear nervous around adults or may act out aggressively, as they deal with the self-doubts and low self-esteem they are feeling. Most of the time children are so confused and conflicted that they do not want to tell anyone and they want to deny that the abuse happened so that they can get beyond it. Ordinarily, instead of transcending what happened to them, victims of abuse bury it deep within where it festers and weakens them emotionally. Common long-term effects of sexual molestation are substance abuse, depression, anger, anxiety, nightmares, self-mutilation, eating disorders and inability to form relationships. The worst possible effect is suicide. Morphing from being a victim to an abuser is not unheard of.

Scores of victims of priest sexual misconduct have spoken about the way they were harmed at the time the abuse was happening as well as in the years that followed. By stopping to hear from some of them we can begin to learn the human toll at the heart of this scandal.

Carol Poppito, 41 years old, who alleges that she was

abused by Father James Smith starting when she was ten or eleven years old and a student in a Catholic elementary school, recounted thirty years later how Smith had warned her, "Don't tell anybody," and "Don't tell your father," a police lieutenant, about the abuse.[64] Father Smith, "everybody's favorite priest" took her out of class several times a year, from the time she was in the fifth or sixth grade until eighth grade, and molested her in the stairwell or an empty nurse's office. Mrs. Poppito said that because of the abuse she does not trust anyone with her children. "I sit in the pouring rain … during their football practices, their lacrosse practices," she said.[65] And deep-seated resentment may prompt her remark, "I would love for my parents to get their tuition back for sending their seven children to Holy Trinity instead of PS 149 to keep us safe."[66]

Leo Clark, a victim of molestation by a priest, says that the sexual abuse that happened to him as a child tormented him well into adulthood. At the time of the abuse and for a while afterward, Clark remembers taking three showers a day to try to make himself feel clean. After the abuse stopped, Clark had trouble sleeping and had difficulty maintaining relationships. He has flashbacks and, once when his abuser's name came up, he reacted in anger, went into a rage and tipped over a table. Now, Mr. Clark sees a therapist and meets in a victim's support group. He says that his main goal is to let go of the past and begin to live a normal life.[67]

Joe Fluette III, also a victim of priest sex abuse, talked about burying the memories of what happened to him deep inside and trying to cope on his own. "I thought I was all alone. I thought I was the only one" Father Desilets had ever touched. Mr. Fluette recounted feeling guilty and troubled about making lowly allegations against a figure of such stature, allegations that seemed, especially to a child, no one was likely to believe. "You can't go against God," he said. Now he realizes that keeping his story buried was counterproductive; by letting people know "what the monster did" he was now helping himself and others.[68]

Another victim of molestation, Carol Desrosiers, successfully sued a priest. She said that when she was abused there was "an element" that hit her soul and made her think that it was God who treated her this way. "It takes an effort to realize, 'No, it was a human being who was the furthest thing from God.'"[69] Explaining the way Ms. Desrosiers was thinking, Laurie Pearlman, a psychologist at the Traumatic Stress Institute in South Windsor, Connecticut, said that abuse is not only a "betrayal by a parent figure," but a robbery of the "spiritual security that another child might be able to find in a belief in God." Pearlman goes on to say:

Sexual abuse can forever alter a young child's view of the world. "To be used as an object to satisfy someone else's need is a profound violation of the self. It's not an act that is over and done with. It will color all of a child's relationships," Pearlman said. "A child is left asking, 'Whom can I trust? Can I trust myself? Am I a worthy person or just an object to be used by others? Am I valuable? Can I control what happens to me?'"[70]

One of the most horrible consequences of being abused is that the abused child can grow up to become a sexually abusing adult. This is what allegedly happened to Robert Malo, who as a youngster was abused by a priest and who years later was convicted of sexually abusing one of his own children. Fearing for the safety of her children, Malo's wife did not want him set free at the end of his jail term because he did not receive counseling in prison and she considered him a continuing threat.[71]

A startling delayed response to being abused is to lash out at the abuser with deadly intent. This is exactly what Dontee Stokes did when he shot his alleged abuser, former priest Maurice Blackwell. Stokes claimed that Blackwell, his mentor, abused him for three years. Stokes never sought professional help and tried to deal with the effects of the abuse on his own. He tended to be angry, to brood, and to struggle with depression. "He slept whenever he could; his family came to call it his 'escape.'"[72] Angered by memories of what had happened to him as well as by knowing that Archbishop Keeler of Baltimore reassigned Father Blackwell in 1993 after the priest completed a counseling program, Stokes shot Blackwell, whose injuries were not life threatening.[73] On December 17, 2002, a jury in Baltimore, Maryland, acquitted Stokes of all felony charges, including murder, reckless endangerment, and assault. Walter A. Brown, Dontee Stoke's lawyer, said the jury agreed with his client's temporary insanity defense. "Dontee pulled the trigger, but others were behind his doing that, including the Catholic Church and Father Blackwell," the lawyer said.[74]

Generalized demoralization

Obviously, the church is experiencing a deep and painful crisis. We could employ an analogy and say that we have examined a patient and diagnosed the existence of multi-organ failure. Our analogy limps, however, because, after we make decisions about CPR and technological interventions, there is nothing to do for the patient with multi-organ failure but wait for nature to take its course. As we know, the church is dying, but it will not die. It will either become more corrupt, become more irrelevant, acquire still more sick symptoms, or it will turn a corner and begin to experience an overall improvement in its condition. How can such a big organization with such deeply entrenched problems begin the long process of recovery?

The key element to be addressed involves the church in its functioning as a bureaucratic institution. Once institutional issues are examined and institutional sins repented, there can be a turnaround for the church as a whole. It is time to look at these issues and discuss how they can be resolved.

Look

This scandal is all the greater precisely because the story has been around so long. In other words, there is simply no excuse for a bishop to not have figured that when he gets one of these cases, the only possible ethical response is to a) remove the priest immediately; b) call the cops; c) make an honest effort to find all the victims; d) deal with the problem publicly, even if that means opening your diocese to further lawsuits; e) treat the kids and the parents – and all the other parishioners – humanely. That this wasn't being done 10 and 15 years after the 1985 Doyle/Mouton/Peterson report and half a dozen years after the bishops in the early 1990s adopted guidelines for dealing with this problem made the story more horrific, not less.

–Carl M. Cannon[75]

We are dealing with a "systemic problem, deeply rooted."
"Don't settle for less than real change." The church needs to
"expose the wound before healing can begin."

–David Clohessy[76]

The underlying scandal is the behavior of bishops. Bishops
are complicit in the moral bankruptcy of the Church.

–Scott Appleby[77]

I n the first section of this book, we stopped to consider what we are dealing with. Now we need to take a long, hard look beneath the surface to determine the causes of the crisis that embroils the Catholic Church. Three issues will be examined in order to get to the bottom of what went wrong: Catholic sexual ethics, accountability of cardinals and bishops, and theological issues.

Catholic sexual ethics

Catholic sexual ethics relies on abstract thinking that is built around the conviction that heterosexual intercourse is a necessary human action because it provides the means to propagate the human race. Heterosexual intercourse can also bring pleasure to participants and, ideally, it bonds them together. Catholic sexual teaching does not object to pleasure for married people and it is in favor of the bonding aspect of sexual relations. The church teaches that emotional and biological connectedness are at the heart of the family, and establishing this connectedness leads to a stable context for raising children.

Catholic sexual ethics places considerable focus on the act of intercourse so that there are absolute condemnations of artificial contraception and direct sterilization because these render intercourse unproductive. The church's regard for the product of conception, the embryo, is absolute. Therefore, the church maintains that the existence of an embryo within the uterus or in the laboratory and the existence of the fetus at any stage of development can never be terminated.

Since premarital and extramarital sex do not provide the same context for procreation as marriage, Catholic teaching rejects both kinds of relationships as immoral. Since masturbation is neither unifying nor procreative, it is forbidden. And since homosexual acts cannot result in conception and since, according to the church's interpretation of natural law, they are not the means that God and nature intended for interpersonal sexual bonding, all homosexual genital acts are assessed as immoral.

Catholic sexual ethics is consistent and straightforward. It is simple, direct and clear. However, the simplicity of Catholic sexual ethics may actually be problematic because this teaching overlooks or avoids significant issues.

An inherent assumption of the Catholic approach to sexual morality is that humans have two parts, a lower part which is instinctual and based in the body, driven by passion, and a higher part which is spiritual or rational, based in the mind and soul, and designed to regulate the lower part. Reason must govern sexual urges so that people will live orderly, sensible lives and so that mature married people who are capable of raising children will conceive them. While heterosexual urges and actions are tolerable as a means to an end, they are somewhat undesirable. There is lingering discomfort in Catholic teaching for heterosexual pleasure because heretical approaches to sex have influenced Catholic teaching since the time of St. Augustine in the fourth century.[78] While the church accepts heterosexual coupling, it maintains that homosexual genital pleasure is never tolerable because it is abnormal, unnatural and evil.

Catholic sexual ethics and difficult cases

There is no flexibility in Catholic sexual ethics, leaving the church with nothing to suggest concerning the difficult cases of contemporary interest. Take the case of Andrea and Russell Yates, noncatholics who obviously did not practice contraception and had five children in quick succession. (Catholic teaching is based on natural law, and is derived from reason. It does not matter whether individuals are Catholic or not, or even if they believe in God because, according to the Catholic take on natural law, its precepts are applicable to all human persons. Catholic officials say that everyone is bound to act according to reason, or natural law. That most noncatholics do not agree with the rules about sexual conduct proposed by Catholic authorities does not prompt them to alter this position. Since natural law would be the basis for deciding questions about the use of contraceptives, in the Yates case, as in all cases, use of contraceptives to prevent conception would be forbidden.) In spite of the fact that Andrea Yates suffered from severe postpartum depression, she and her husband continued to have noncontracepted sexual relations. They wanted to keep on having babies. After Andrea Yates drowned her five children in Texas in 2001, her insanity and/or the refusal of Mr. and Mrs. Yates to use contraception or undergo sterilization were cited as causes of the children's deaths.

According to Catholic teaching, even postpartum depression as severe as that suffered by Andrea Yates does not constitute sufficient reason for recourse to sterilization or artificial birth control. People who consider the church's doctrine in the context of this case are inclined to concur with those who argue that Russell Yates should have made certain that his mentally ill, depressed wife did not get pregnant, thus putting themselves at variance with official Catholic teaching. They would locate a weakness in a system that derives absolute prohibitions from reason and makes no exceptions based on real people who suffer from psychiatric illness. The church's solution to the Yates' dilemma, that they not have intercourse if they did not want to conceive, is unacceptable to most people because it ignores the feelings that prompt married people to engage in sexual relations.

Married people who cannot get pregnant present

another problematic case; their desire to use technology collides with Catholic sexual teaching. The church maintains that those couples that choose artificial insemination or in vitro fertilization in order to achieve parenthood violate natural law and become parents through unethical acts. While these couples and their loved ones look at children conceived through laboratory assistance as miracles of modern medicine, unchanging Catholic moral teaching insists that this means of conception is against both God's law and human nature.

Most young people today are hesitant to make a commitment to marriage. They do not want to make a mistake; they want to feel certain about their relationship before they pronounce vows. They have witnessed divorce and understand how children in divorced families suffer. In a great many cases these young people decide to live together. Parents usually are not pleased when their children choose this arrangement rather than marriage. Elders register disapproval while trying to encourage couples that live together to pronounce the life-altering promises contained in the marriage ceremony.

The Catholic Church, unlike parents, registers only disapproval of cohabitation. In the eyes of the church living together is "living in sin;" it constitutes fornication and is immoral. Since church leaders tend not to communicate with young Catholics who cohabitate, there is little or no exchange between them. If there were to be dialogue, it is unlikely that young people would grant that the church's arguments against their living arrangements are more persuasive than the arguments they hold in favor of them. Perhaps young people are simply rationalizing and they have uncritically appropriated the mores of the sexual revolution. And maybe the thinking of the Catholic Church is far more persuasive than young people are willing to admit. The truth is probably someplace in between, a compromise in which young people acknowledge pitfalls inherent in cohabitation and church leaders recognize that there is wisdom in not making a commitment before partners are able to do so without reservation.

In terms of pushing the envelope on abortion, when the situation of the pregnant woman is truly horrific the majority of people seem willing to allow the procedure. The so-called 1992 X Case in Ireland captured media attention and led to an unprecedented decision by the Supreme Court of Ireland. A fourteen-year-old girl was raped by her girlfriend's father and became pregnant. When her parents discovered what had happened they acceded to her wishes to be taken to London to get an abortion. (Abortion is not performed in Ireland.) As they were making travel arrangements, the parents contacted police to ask what kinds of tissue they should bring back to use in a trial against the attacker. Through the phone call police learned that the parents were going to take their daughter to London to have an abortion. The police explained that the family could not leave Ireland as it was against the law to leave the country for an abortion. The pregnant teenager then said that she would commit suicide if she had to continue with the pregnancy. The case became widely known and the drama played out in the media. Public opinion was largely with the family. The thinking was that, in this horrible situation, the girl should be allowed to go ahead with the abortion. The force of this opinion caused the Irish Supreme Court to make an exception for this victim and allow her parents to take the youngster to London for the procedure.

In this case the principle upheld by the Catholic Church—that a fetus, no matter what its origin, is a vulnerable human life and ought not to be terminated—seemed less persuasive than the distress of the girl who was raped. In other words, the exigency of circumstances held more sway than rational argument.

Gay Catholic men find themselves in an especially difficult predicament. If they choose to abstain from sex, they conform their behavior to biblical injunctions against same sex coupling and they abide by Catholic teaching that they practice lifelong celibacy. As it stands, only a very small percent of gay Catholic men choose to make a commitment to abstinence. Those who do not make such an election select from among three options. They become promiscuous, having sex with a few or a lot of partners. Or, they enter into an open relationship, having sex with a primary partner and others. Or, they choose a committed, monogamous union. While official Catholic teaching opposes this third option, many Catholic moral and pastoral theologians favor it because they think monogamy can be achieved and partners in monogamous unions stand a good chance of attaining spiritual and psychosexual maturity. Furthermore, they question the ability of gays to observe the restraints contained in a commitment to lifelong celibacy and worry about risks to individuals who fail in this commitment.

Within the elaboration of official Catholic teaching, passion and the subconscious receive little attention and the human need for physical intimacy is inadequately considered. In contrast, theologians who dissent from official teaching base their objections on an understanding of human persons that includes consideration of psychological factors. They conclude that for the vast majority of homosexuals a life of total celibacy is impossible. A homosexual person who resolves to be celibate but fails is likely to engage in impulsive sexual acts. Succumbing to temptation usually entails anonymous, promiscuous encounters. Those who choose promiscuity or open relationships are also likely to engage in anonymous, promiscuous sex. From a moral point of view, such sex, if the result of giving in to a strong temptation, would not be grievously sinful because passion lessens a person's moral culpability. On the other hand, in theory, if individuals deliberately choose homosexual behavior within a committed relationship, they would be guilty of grave sin because they purposely intend to engage in homoerotic actions. Psychology teaches that promiscuous casual sex is impersonal and demeaning, and it undermines a person's sense of self-esteem. And, from the point of view of physical well being in the age of AIDS, anonymous, promiscuous sex is very dangerous. Psychological and medical data inform the dissenting opinion, leading to a compromise. The hierarchy, basing its moral teaching on the structure of the sexual act, cannot consider compromising and thus dismisses the physical and psychological factors that inform the dissenting opinion.

One result of the church's position against tolerance of gay sex and gay couples is that homophobia is not countered by Catholic leaders and the church does not play a significant role in decrying this form of prejudice. Homophobia is a strong and irrational fear of homosexuals and homosexuality. Homophobia was the motive for the 1998 murder of Matthew Shepherd, a Wyoming college student who was beaten almost to death and left to die on a fence. Homophobia is what keeps gay sons from ever disclosing their sexual orientation to their fathers and what causes fathers to say "I wish he were dead" when they discover their son's orientation.

In the context of the incidence of sex abuse by priests in the Catholic Church, it is essential that bishops address the issue of repressed homosexual tendencies that erupt in the sexual abuse of young boys (pedophilia) and, more frequently, in abuse of boys 14 to 17 years old (ephebophilia).[79] Sexual abuse of male children has happened in the Catholic Church even though the church condemns all homosexual acts, and priests have promised to be celibate. Church leaders need to learn if there is a connection between the church's taboo against homosexual acts and the compulsive drive that results in abuse of boys by priests. Do priest sex offenders molest children because of their repressed urges? Did these urges lead these men to the priesthood? In other words, during their adolescent years, did priest molesters suspect that they were gay and react to this suspicion with dread because the church holds homosexual behavior in contempt? Did they then seek to repress their sexual identity and their urges by embracing a celibate lifestyle in which they pledged to forgo all sexual acts? In spite of their intention to be celibate, did they succumb to temptation and prey on boys because they could not resist the urges, which they never wanted to acknowledge?

Appraisals of Catholic sexual ethics

Conservative forces within Catholicism want to hold onto the traditional approach to sexual morality that does not compromise principles and that maintains absolute rules for human conduct. They are especially interested in continuing to reject abortion and homosexuality as well as other forbidden sexual actions as absolutely immoral. Frequently, a vitriolic disgust with homosexuality is apparent. Conservatives think that what liberals propose would result in abandoning reasonable standards and result in moral chaos.

Liberal forces in the Catholic Church want to refocus the church's teaching so that it is not centered on the heterosexual act of intercourse or the rights of an embryo or fetus. They want an evaluation of the circumstances of people faced with ethical conflicts while not abandoning traditional standards derived from reason. Additionally, liberals want more attention paid to the sexual maturation process humans undergo, with more consideration given to what is appropriate behavior at various stages of development. For example, they think that masturbation by adolescents signifies a normal part of growing up and should not be categorized as an immoral action.

As church leaders struggle to make children safe within its confines they need to look at the foundations of their Catholic morality and affirm or revise these foundations. This is a multifaceted task, a radical one made more difficult by the fact that there are deep differences of opinion about whether or not there is a problem with the way official teaching is formulated.

Conservatives within the church want to silence dissent, promulgate traditional rule-and act-centered sexual morality, and emphasize the responsibilities of bishops to teach according to the catechism[80] and the laity to obey. They want to strengthen the influence of the church in the lives of young Catholics so as to diminish the role played by secular forces such as the entertainment industry which trivializes the meaning of the marriage commitment and promotes the idea that sex is for recreation. They are opposed to abortion in all circumstances. Especially they reject attempts to normalize or neutralize homosexual genital activity, holding on to a strong condemnation of all instances of this activity regardless of circumstances.

Conservatives suggest a connection between the child sex abuse crisis in the church and a softening of Catholic attitudes toward homosexuality. Because the church admits large numbers of homosexual candidates to its seminaries and seems increasingly tolerant of their homosexual orientation, conservatives reason that church leaders have contributed to a situation in which priests molest children. Since most abuse is of adolescent boys, the same leaders who welcome gay men to the priesthood enable these men to be in a privileged position in relation to the children they abuse. Therefore, conservatives argue that were seminaries to reject homosexual candidates and homosexual behavior, the child abuse problem would be largely eliminated.

Centrists and liberals think that Catholic sexual ethics needs to change, but their understanding of how this reworking should be accomplished is totally different from that of conservatives. Since sexuality is a personal matter and since sexual relations are interpersonal, the basic premise from which the centrist-liberal argument is constructed is that Catholic sexual ethics should move away from the concentration on acts and the structures of acts toward a consideration of how persons prosper or suffer from their sexuality and the sexual acts in which they engage. Beyond this, progressives want church leaders to focus more on circumstances and the motivations of people who make sexual choices.

The rational, abstract system favored by Catholic tradition emphasizes the role of the intellect and the will in respect to the sexual choices people make. Homosexual genital acts are forbidden because they do not conform to nature. Since church teaching takes little or no account of the circumstances, i.e., whether sex is with a minor or an adult, social and legal taboos against adults having sex with minors are not emphasized in the Catholic setting. Those who are socialized by the church, such as seminarians and priests, may not realize the relevance of this distinction, putting innocent children in peril.

Given that the Catholic approach to sexual ethics is to teach that heterosexual intercourse in marriage is normative and chastity in all other contexts is required, until recently church leaders have not devoted attention to educating priests, lay adults or school-age children about the dynamics of sexual abuse and how to identify and prevent sexual molestation. Since priests commit to celibacy, it has been assumed that they do not need instruction in this regard. Hence, education about boundaries and being taught what "good touching" and "bad touching" consist of has been lacking. Some people and cultures are more demonstrative regarding physical signs of affection than others, but not even this matter has been covered. Certainly, if there is no touch, the possibility of a priest's being accused of sexual molestation diminishes almost completely. Instances of sexual molestation that do not involve touch include exhibitionism in which a person exposes genitals to another or watches erotic videos. Failure to discuss and differentiate in regard to these matters has constituted negligence on the part of those responsible for the education of priests.

Additionally, because of the way sexual ethics is taught in the Catholic Church, the vulnerability of children goes unexamined, as does the dynamics of relationships involving the powerful and the powerless. People who have suffered sexual abuse tell us that what makes it easy for a priest to molest a youngster is the priest's collar, a sign that marks him as a trusted guide who belongs to God's realm. Priests, parents, and children need to understand that no one is allowed to violate sexual boundaries that separate adults, including priests, from children. Children are to be respected, protected and not harmed; they are not sexual objects to be used to gratify adult sexual appetites.

Catholic parents have acted from the mistaken assumption that priests do not have sex. How many priests abstain from sex? How many priests are sexually active, and in what does that activity consist? Church leadership can no longer justify keeping silent on this subject. They alone are in a position to compile data that would answer these questions. Bishops are responsible for recruiting candidates for priesthood and staffing parishes with priests. During candidates' seminary preparation as well as after their ordination, bishops exercise authority over them. Bishops are responsible for keeping or dismissing problem seminarians or priests. Therefore, bishops bear responsibility for ordaining unfit candidates; reassigning sexual molesters rests squarely on bishops' shoulders.

In light of the way they function within the Catholic

Church, there are two tasks that bishops, and bishops alone, can carry out that will result in significant progress. In this process bishops will uncover heretofore-unknown data that can be used to inform the future course of priest selection and supervision.

First, bishops need to address the issue of repressed homosexual tendencies that erupt in the sexual abuse of boys.[81] They can do this by talking with men who have been removed from the priesthood because of credible charges against them. Therapists at such facilities as Saint Luke's in Maryland also have pertinent information. Reporters and lawyers do not know the names of molesters or how to contact them. Even if reporters could reach therapists, those who work for the Catholic Church would probably not be willing to divulge what they know. Bishops, however, have access to relevant data, and obtaining it is crucial. If there is a correlation between repressed homosexuality by adolescents who want to be priests and compulsive urges to abuse minors which surface at a later date, the correlation can then be identified and described. The articulation of a psychosexual profile could provide guidelines in screening candidates for priesthood.

Opening up this issue might reveal that deficiencies in church teaching have led sex abuser priests to such a degree of homophobia that they can tolerate themselves only if they deny their own sexual orientation. If this turns out to be the case, church leaders might decide to reexamine their presentation of sexual ethics, reevaluating whether church teaching about homosexual orientation and homosexual acts should be reformulated so as not to cause disgust and dread in those directly affected by it.

By delivering information about patterns that are likely to occur in the psychological development of priest-abusers, bishops can advance the understanding of how potential abusers can identify themselves and seek help before they do harm. Additionally, nonabuser priests and other interested parties will begin to understand why priest sexual molesters behave as they do and will have clues enabling them to register appropriate responses or suspicions.

In its teaching, church leaders situate sexual morality within individual and family contexts. The church sidesteps social and civic questions regarding the safety of children and it leaves abuser-priests alone to cope with their criminal desires. Perhaps they molest children because they cannot face what they feel and they lack social skills to establish sexual relationships with adults. The thought of entering into adult sex does not even occur because the priest molester could not manage that relational demand. Facing this reality is disconcerting because it seems outrageous to address the issue of the sexual maturation of priests who are supposed to abstain from sex. More outrageous, however, would be to bypass this issue and keep our heads in the sand, thereby not addressing what could be the root of the problem.

In concluding this section, the centrist-liberal coalition maintains that the contemporary Catholic Church grudgingly admits that people have psychological, emotional and hormonal sexual needs, but the church continues to deal with motivation about sexual conduct from an abstract, rational perspective that does not take real life situations into account. Conservatives, on the other hand, point to waffling about the cogency of the church's rational approach to sexual morality as a major cause of the chaos in the church. They contend that the Catholic Church needs to reassert absolute standards of sexual morality based in reason. Catholic bishops in the United States need to look beneath the surface of competing opinions and reach consensus on the contours of a fully adequate teaching on sexual ethics.

Accountability of Cardinals and Bishops

Accountability means answering for decisions one makes or fails to make. Hence, we speak of "being held accountable" and, in terms of the crisis in the Catholic Church, it is the cardinals and bishops who are being held accountable for policies they executed. In the Catholic Church hierarchy, bishops, cardinals and the pope have jurisdiction over priests lower in rank as well as over the laity. Since it is the bishops who have been entrusted with oversight of the church, an explanation falls on their shoulders when the church is in disarray.

For most of the twentieth century the laity assumed that members of the hierarchy were doing a good job. Given the pedestals on which cardinals and bishops were placed, it would have been inconceivable to think otherwise. The pope is the successor of Saint Peter; cardinals and bishops carry staffs as a sign that they have been cast in the biblical role of shepherds. The laity believed they were in good hands.

Lay Catholics have been slow to recognize that church leaders have not been good shepherds. From the 1985 Gauthe case[82] through the major cases of the nineties involving people like James Porter (Massachusetts, 1993),[83] Edward Pipala (New York, 1993)[84] and the 1997 Rudolf Kos case in Dallas, Texas,[85] the laity was inclined to accept the explanations of bishops who had reassigned serial molesters, giving bishops the benefit of the doubt that they had acted in good conscience based on the advice of mental health professionals. With the events of 2002, however, these explanations began to sound hollow and men and women started objecting to the way the hierarchy manages the church. And they began holding their shepherds accountable.

To whom should American cardinals and bishops,

and, ultimately, the pope, be held accountable? And of what should this accountability consist? Let us look at eight groups to whom members of the hierarchy need to exercise accountability and consider the specifics of how accountability would be exercised with regard to each.

1. Accountability to victims of clergy sexual abuse

Accountability to people who were molested by priests should begin with an acknowledgement of what they have suffered and continue to suffer. Part of healing comes from stating what happened; in this interest, members of the hierarchy need to listen to victims and stop efforts designed to keep them quiet. Learn from Sonia C. Solomonson who writes, "Having someone hear and believe the story of abuse is a critical foundation for healing. It's especially important that someone who represents the church believes the story. The scandals rocking the Roman Catholic Church in recent months bring reminders that victims who feel neglected are more likely to seek justice in the courts."[86]

The Catholic hierarchy spent money on settlements that required confidentiality of victims. This money changed hands in order to preserve the reputation of the church. But in 2002, the drum roll of cases frustrated that goal. The fact that the strategy has been unsuccessful, however, is not the reason to discontinue confidentiality agreements; the reason to abandon these arrangements is to focus on the needs of victims and put their interests first.

Bishops need to admit to victims that they have been inadequate personnel managers of their priests and to admit their negligence. At the least, known instances of continued abuse by reassigned priests point to a serious lack of vigilance on the part of bishops. At worst, offending priests who were reassigned may provide examples of complicity by bishops who chose to minimize the horror of sexual abuse and to disregard the nature of the crime in the interest of staffing needs.

How much money are victims of sexual assault by priests entitled to? This is a loaded question. They certainly are entitled to sufficient funds to pay for counseling, loss of productivity, and punitive damages as determined by lawyers or courts. When seeking justice, victims should not have to endure the questioning of their integrity, or listen to suggestions that "they are just trying to make money." Anyone who knows what a typical victim has endured knows how insulting and deceitful are these remarks. Additionally, church leaders should instruct lawyers not to engage in hardball tactics in questioning victims. Victim-survivors have suffered enough and it is not their credibility that is on the line.

When victims meet with attorneys representing the church or the church's insurance companies, they expect to be treated with respect and compassion. In the past, that was frequently not the case. Consider, for example, the abusive litigation tactics which involved the archdiocese of Philadelphia. The archdiocese countersued the parents of a man who said that a priest had sexually abused him. The archdiocese's theory was that the parents were also liable for endangering their son by allowing him to spend time with the priest in the face of warning signs. Facing criticism for taking this position, the archdiocese blamed its insurance company for the decision to counter-sue.[87] Bishops should realize that such treatment is unacceptable and they must put a stop to it. They are accountable for the tactics of lawyers in their employ and need to answer for the harsh treatment of victim-survivors.

The most important thing that bishops can do to be accountable to victims is to make absolutely certain that offending priests never again harm anyone. This is the primary concern of survivors; the bishops who let them down in the first instance by leaving offending priests in place or reassigning them should once and for all break the cycle by preventing priest molesters from ever again exercising ministry.

The Catholic bishops of the United States promised to take this step in Dallas, Texas, on June 14, 2002 when they voted 239 to 13 to adopt the Charter for the Protection of Children and Young People. Their task now is to make absolutely certain that this policy is more than words on paper. Victim-survivors have seen policies adopted before and still abuse continued. As this new era begins, victims are insisting on the transparent accountability of the American bishops. David Clohessy, director of a survivor network, expressed skepticism about how thoroughly the new policies would be carried out. Speaking to a reporter in Dallas, Clohessy recalled 1992, when the bishops' conference passed a previous policy on child abuse, and said, "Those statements looked impressive too."[88] (Amendments to the charter enacted by the Vatican will be considered in the final section of this book entitled Listen.)

2. Accountability to lay Catholics

Lay Catholics have been far more patient than called for, entrusting oversight of the church to the hierarchy with the naïve expectation that bishops would do a competent job. This has not been the case. Lay people are now waking up and demanding accountability. Of what would this accountability consist? According to Bishop Wilton Gregory, President of the United States Conference of Catholic bishops, "Roman Catholics would like their leaders to trade the church's culture of secrecy for openness and accountability. The first obligation is to make such matters known. The second is to set transparent rules that hold the church responsible for its mistakes."[89] To the laity this means that church administration and record keeping will no longer be obscure and that we will have a way to learn what is going on. It means, further, that if bishops do not disclose financial or administrative information, there will be a process that lay people can engage in to find out what they want to know. The conspiracy of silence and the guiding principle that Father knows best have to be laid to rest.

Beyond this, the laity still questions whether or not they have been fully informed about the extent of the sex abuse scandal. We have been provided with information from the media and lawyers, but we do not know what the bishops know, which is probably more than what the reporters and courts have told us. The laity wants their bishops to level with them: How many kids? How much money? Where did the money for the settlements come from? How many reassignments? How many priests are still ministering who have been guilty of abusing our children? Are we mistaken as we wait for the other shoe to drop?

Accountability means that both information and motivation are open to examination. Bishops need to stand before the people in their dioceses and render accounts. Are the bishops merely paying lip service to the idea of lay involvement? It is obvious that the sex abuse scandal would not have been nearly so extensive if lay people shared insight and oversight with bishops. Lay people are now beginning to ask how the system of church administration is changing or will change to allow for lay insight and oversight that complements the jurisdiction of bishops. Those of us who lived through Vatican II and who watched as parish councils and diocesan advisory boards were formed in the 1970s and rendered impotent in the 1980s wonder how the bishops want the laity to participate. The prevailing attitude of skepticism was well expressed by Margaret O'Brien Steinfels when she said, "This scandal has brought home to laypeople how essentially powerless they are to affect its outcome. What layperson isn't brought up short in realizing (40 years after Vatican II with its promise of consultation and collaboration) that our only serious leverage is money? That, itself, is a scandal."[90] Bishop accountability to lay Catholics demands that bishops provide specific information about what they want us to do and how, moving forward, things are going to be different.

3. Accountability to "good" priests

After victim-survivors, those who have suffered most from the way bishops have handled sex abuse cases are the "good" priests, unquestionably the overwhelming majority. Since bishops have not provided an accurate account of how many priests have molested minors, we do not know how many priests fall into the category of "good priests." But reliable estimates are that the number is likely more than ninety-eight percent. The vast majority of priests are, therefore, in a very unfortunate situation. Because of publicity surrounding this scandal people are aware that some priests have molested children. Molesters do not wear signs, so that no one knows if a priest is a sexual molester or not. A popular idea that has taken hold is that *any* priest may be a molester. This is logically true but it is likewise logically true that *any* person may be a child molester. Since, at present, there is not an association of child molestation with other professions, however, people do not look askance at members of other professions the way they do at priests. Since the number of priest molesters is very small, indicating that there is but a minuscule chance that an individual priest may have committed a crime of this type or may be inclined to do so, good priests are in a terrible situation and are under suspicion. In the current environment most priests feel that people are looking at them, that people are mistrustful of them. These priests are correct; they are not being paranoid.

Part of the accountability that bishops owe to faithful priests is to act decisively and immediately to permanently remove offending priests and to make certain no man credibly accused of molesting a child continues to function as a priest. After people believe that this policy is in effect, we will be able to enter a new era in which the ministry of worthy priests is not shadowed in suspicion.

In addition to restoring credibility to priestly ministry, members of the hierarchy also need to be open with priests, fully disclosing to them the entire scope of the sex abuse crisis. Priests deserve to be in the loop. Pastors who have unwittingly been assigned priest molesters in the past deserve a sincere apology, as well as assurance that in the future this type of egregious negligence will not be repeated. The disturbing case of Father Eugene O'Sullivan is a case in point. In 1984, Father O'Sullivan pleaded guilty in Boston to molesting an altar boy and was placed on five years' probation and ordered not to have contact with children. In 1985, Father O'Sullivan was transferred to New Jersey where then-bishop Theodore McCarrick of the diocese of Metuchen assigned him to four different parishes before he was recalled to Boston in 1993. A report in *The New York Times* about his case reads, "three of the parishes were not told about the 1984 conviction."[91] This is an unconscionable position for a bishop to put a pastor and parishioners in. It must not happen again.

Since priests work and live in close proximity, they are the ones who are most likely to witness unacceptable conduct by offender priests. Bishops need to set up procedures by which suspicions can be reported. This is a sensitive matter in that if suspicions are substantiated the result will be termination of ministry. Priests and bishops need to work together to enforce compliance. Because false or inaccurate accusations can be made, cooperation of good priests needs to be examined carefully; their support for a procedure, which involves them in monitoring each other's conduct, is key to its success.

Bishops repeatedly contend that the issue of sexual molestation by priests is not connected to the church requirement that priests be celibate. Bishops argue that celibacy is a gift from God, which enables priests to be at the total service of the church. They reason that those who abuse minors are mentally ill and act out of a sick compulsion that has nothing to do with celibacy. They state further that the celibacy requirement of the Catholic priesthood does not attract sexually dysfunctional people who enter the priesthood in order to avoid dealing with their problems. And bishops maintain that the incidence of sex abuse of children in the priesthood is no greater than in other professions. Critics of the bishops disagree with their reasoning and say that the issue of who is attracted to celibacy needs to be honestly evaluated. Since no one knows better about their attitude on celibacy than priests themselves, it makes sense for the hierarchy to consult with priests in exploring this matter.

Furthermore, the issue of the sexual orientation of priests needs to be confronted. What percentage is heterosexual? What percentage is homosexual? If there is a larger percentage of gays in the priesthood than in the general population, why is this the case? Is celibacy possible for priests of both orientations? Is it harder to be chaste for those of one orientation or the other? What are priests' sexual urges and how do they deal with them? How have priests managed to deal with their needs for physical intimacy? These questions need to be addressed by bishops and priests in honest, open, humble forums. While bishops may be reluctant to open this very personal and highly controversial area to discussion and priests may be distressed about talking of these matters, a thorough investigation needs to occur so that the priestly state, in its current celibate form, can meet the test of credibility. And bishops, by opening the discussion, can meet one expectation in regard to their obligation to accountability. If the results of an examination reveal that celibacy is a stumbling block for the majority of men who are priests, then bishops should try to convince the Vatican to revise this requirement.

A final point of accountability for bishops is to take into consideration the fact that in 2002 more than 325 priests were ordered to discontinue ministry because they abused children. There are approximately 46,000 priests in the United States, not enough to staff all openings. By reducing the number of priests, bishops add to the responsibilities of those remaining. Adding more work to men who are already stretched thin and perhaps demoralized is not a workable solution. It will increase the burnout suffered by good priests. In the interest of responsible management, bishops need to resist the temptation to ignore the reality of the priest shortage. It is their responsibility to plan for staffing Catholic institutions and they are to be held accountable in this regard.

4. Accountability to each other

There are fewer than four hundred bishops and cardinals in the United States. These men are members of an elite club and, prior to the sex abuse scandal, they enjoyed considerable prestige. Many of them also conducted themselves as though they were superior to ordinary people. This is changing, and the demand that the hierarchy be accountable is the first evidence of the change.

Cardinals and bishops do have important administrative and pastoral roles, and the way the church is set up, they are in charge. Because the problems they face are daunting, it is all the more important that members of the hierarchy support one another. They should offer counsel and emotional support to each other. For the good of the church, when they suspect that one of their own is incompetent or negligent, they should seek to have that person step aside or take steps to have him removed. The Catholic hierarchy has a few very prestigious positions held by cardinals and archbishops and many lower ones held by bishops. Often those who become bishops are ambitious and want to advance to archbishop or cardinal. There is competition in the hierarchy, attempts to outdo each other and impress Vatican officials who make decisions about promotions.

Competition is part of human nature but, in the Catholic hierarchy, it functions in a negative way, preventing cooperation and collaboration. Notre Dame history professor Scott Appleby notes the corrosive quality of the competition. In addressing the bishops, he said, "...you are divided among yourselves, and some of you even take pleasure or comfort in the travails of other bishops."[92] What should be done to counter competition and the division it engenders is unclear. There is no question, however, that this behavior should be addressed in order to improve the climate for shared governance.

Another problem facing the hierarchy is the existence of factions within it. Bishops and cardinals appointed by Pope Paul VI, before 1978, tend to be more liberal than those appointed by Pope John Paul II. The latter group has marginalized the former group. Within the group appointed by John Paul II there are also factions. Some want a very strict interpretation of doctrine and morality and favor a church consisting of fewer Catholics who are more devout and more compliant with Catholic moral teaching. Others see the complexity of modern life and want the church to be more responsive to people who are struggling to live upright Christian lives. Whatever group an individual bishop belongs to, given the present needs of the church, factionalism needs to be put aside and an emphasis has to be placed on working together to make the church a credible institution. In view of the fact that bishops insist on the need for lay collaboration, the hierarchy should ask lay panels to evaluate their performance and should ask the laity to recommend dismissal of bishops when there is evidence of grievous negligence in the conduct of their office.

5. Accountability to the pope and curia

Professor Alberto Melloni, a history professor and member of the John XXIII Foundation in Bologna, Italy, criticized American Catholic leaders who "came to Rome (in April 2002) like kids asking grandpa, 'What should I do?'"[93] It is a mistake to approach the pope and members of the curia as though they are elders who should be protected from information they do not want to hear or as though they have ready answers for the problems of the American church. The American hierarchy needs to engage Rome in straight talk about the crisis that embroils the church. It is a major crisis, the worst ever faced by the Catholic Church in the United

States. Now is the time for American Catholic leaders to take the initiative and tell the Vatican not only about the horrible wrong that was done but also about the deeply rooted systemic faults that need to be corrected.

Just as the American hierarchy has been woefully slow to react to this crisis, so has the response of Rome been deficient. The pope has been slow even to mention the sex abuse crisis and apparently he has not come to grips with the underlying causes of the terrible situation. In this, John Paul II has not been a good shepherd. As painful as it might be for the pope, many issues such as celibacy, the priest shortage, the dynamics of the American hierarchy and the deficits of Catholic sexual ethics need to be put on the table for a full and frank look at elements at the root of this crisis.

6. Accountability to priest molesters

In the context of the sex abuse crisis, the people most to be admired are the victim-survivors and those most to be pitied are the priest molesters. The hierarchy is accountable to these criminals, too. If the church and the priesthood played some role in creating these abusers, bishops need to identify how it was that the church was at fault and correct the problematic dynamics. There are strong bonds among ordained men and the existence of these bonds is one of the reasons why bishops harbored sexual molesters. Accountability demands that bishops recognize that abusers are individuals who, by virtue of their actions, have forfeited their right to exercise ministry. The bishops who ordained these men and conferred on them a trustworthy and exalted rank now need to obtain treatment for them so that they can learn how to control their urges and then find places of confinement and supervision so that they will never again be in situations in which they can harm minors. It will be easier for bishops when priest molesters are prosecuted by the criminal justice system and judges make decisions about prisons and conditions of probation. For priest-molesters whose victims cannot utilize the justice system because statutes of limitation have expired, hierarchical accountability requires that bishops arrange for lifelong supervision of these offenders. In that way, the safety of minors will not be compromised. A huge problem remains involving men who cannot be prosecuted because accusations against them are too old and who resign or are removed from the priesthood. Who protects society from them? The bishops need to open this question to discussion so that a responsible resolution can occur.

7. Accountability to law enforcement agencies

Bishops are members of society just like everyone else. As such, bishops are accountable to render to Caesar the things that are Caesar's. One of the functions of society is to protect the vulnerable, and children are among the most vulnerable members of the human community. Bishops should consider themselves bound by the rules and conventions of society that have been established for the protection of children. *Washington Post* columnist Charles Krauthammer writes concerning bishops and sex abuse cases, "where is the realization of the crime, the violation of the norms and laws of the larger society? Indeed, where is the realization of the larger society?" Krauthamer goes on to say that the scandal has been portrayed as a crisis within the church, but that is a lesser issue: "The major crisis lies not within but without. It is between church and state. It is rooted in the sense of separation, of extrajudicial status, that the American Catholic Church has arrogated for itself for decades when faced with allegations of sexual criminality."[94]

Accountability of bishops as citizens includes cooperating with law enforcement authorities by identifying priests who are accused of sexual misconduct as well as turning over files containing records of past accounts of molestation. When victims come to pastors or bishops with accusations of abuse, they should be told to file complaints with the police. If this had been done during the past quarter century, the church would not be facing the fiscal crisis that exists today. Church leaders cannot undo damage to the church's reputation but they can make credibility a priority going forward. To do this, they need to admit their obligation to be accountable to secular law enforcement authorities.

The bishops acknowledged this requirement in the charter they adopted in Dallas in June 2002:

> Article 4. Dioceses/eparchies will report an allegation of sexual abuse of a person who is a minor to the public authorities. They will cooperate in their investigation in accord with the law of the jurisdiction in question. Dioceses/eparchies will cooperate with public authorities about reporting in cases when the person is no longer a minor. In every instance, dioceses/eparchies will advise victims of their right to make a report to public authorities and will support this right.[95]

Now the bishops need to keep their word.

8. Accountability to members of U.S. society

At the bishop's meeting in Dallas in June 2002, Cardinal Francis George spoke about difficulties faced by the Catholic Church in the United States. He said that U.S. culture is predominantly secular Protestant and that it is simultaneously self-righteous and decadent. There is some truth to this, but, given the crisis created by the Catholic hierarchy, the characteristics of self-righteousness and decadence can aptly be applied to Catholic leadership as well. Trying to turn the tables so that negative aspects of society are emphasized while issues of the church are avoided will not work. The Catholic hierarchy holds administrative responsibility for the Catholic Church. The church is one of many important institutions in society. U.S. society is not perfect and it is corrupt in many regards, but so is the church. Bishops need to focus on the corruption in their own house. They are accountable for cleaning it up. The hierarchy will accomplish nothing by seeking to deflect attention to the social ills of the nation.

Theological Issues

In this section we look beneath the surface of theological formulations to understand what went awry so that we can determine what needs to be changed. Theology is faith seeking understanding. Theological reflection challenges us to understand how the church should function within the context of beliefs in God and Jesus as well as biblical wisdom. Theology requires that we consider how the insights of faith held by Catholics prompt us to proceed in response to the sex scandal in the church. Three areas of theology that are relevant to hierarchical accountability and rebuilding the credibility of Catholicism are theology of the church, theology of priesthood and theology of the laity. We consider each in turn.

Theology of the Church

We could say that the Catholic Church began almost two thousand years ago when the apostles began to preach Jesus' message of good news to the poor, release to captives, (Luke 4:18) and the imminence of the reign of God (Mark 1:15). Tradition holds that Pentecost is the birthday of the church because on that occasion Jesus' followers felt empowered by the Holy Spirit to proclaim this message. From the Upper Room in Jerusalem on that first Pentecost through the early centuries of the Christian era those who believed in Jesus carried his message to more and more places. Leaders instituted ministries in response to the needs of various communities. Jesus did not leave Saint Peter with a blueprint for the church. The apostles and their successors conferred together and used their discretion to provide teaching, preaching, worship, and service to local churches. During the first two hundred years of its existence the offices of bishop, deacon and presbyter (priest) took shape as Christian leadership roles. At the outset, according to University of Notre Dame theologian Richard McBrien, the "organizational, or ministerial component" of the early churches "was for the sake of the mission of the Church, i. e., for service and not for domination."[96]

Tradition, following the New Testament, holds that Peter was considered first among the apostles and that Peter eventually presided over the church of Rome. The office of pope gradually evolved and its location was set in Rome. At the very beginning, Christian thought and customs were influenced mainly by Judaism because Jesus was a Jew, the apostles and most believers were Jews, and the scriptures revered by them were those of the Hebrew Bible. With the spread of Christianity throughout the Mediterranean area, some Greeks began to follow Jesus' teachings and Greek influences melded with Jewish ones so that the thinking of church leaders began to reflect insights of Greek philosophy. Both Jewish and Greek influences continued as the church grew.

A significant early event in Christian history was the conversion of the Emperor Constantine in the fourth century and his decision to make Christianity the official religion of the Roman Empire. This changed the status of Christians from outsiders to honored citizens and it made the church and state allies.

Starting with the Middle Ages and continuing to the present, the culture of Western Europe has had a pronounced influence on Catholic Christianity. The Catholic hierarchy appropriated ranks and signs of office from ancient feudal lords and monarchs. A theological challenge facing today's church is to divest itself of medieval accretions that deter Catholic leaders from modeling the spirit of the apostles. The Catholic hierarchy needs to be in dialogue with historical and New Testament scholarship in order to begin to understand what changes of attitude and practice are needed. The aim of the bishops should be to implement a culture and organizational structure for the church that is directed towards evangelization and service. Since the present culture is closed in on itself and the hierarchy has been unable to credibly administer the church, there is no question about the urgency of this task.

A professor at Saint Peter's College and a newspaper columnist, Raymond Schroth, S. J., suggests that bishops attend a "penance service in Yankee Stadium. There the bishops would put aside their embroidered vestments and pointed hats and melt down their crosiers and replace them with wooden sticks and burn documents in which they are called 'your eminence.'"[97] The trappings associated with the offices of bishop, cardinal, and pope mark holders of these offices as having more in common with medieval monarchs than with the disciples who governed the early church. One of the reasons Vatican II was summoned in 1962 was to unmask the clericalism, juridicism and triumphalism that infected the Catholic hierarchy and prevented church leadership from conducting their offices with the simplicity and sincerity that should characterize their conduct. Sadly, the goal of Vatican II has not yet been reached and the situation forty years later may be worse than it was at the beginning of the council.

Clericalism means that bishops and priests hold the power and authority in the Catholic Church and that these "men of God" are superior to lay people. *Juridicism* means rigidity and preoccupation with rules, laws and rubrics to the detriment of fostering the life-giving spirit that ought to be at the heart of Christianity. *Triumphalism* is the tendency toward an arrogant attitude that proclaims that the Catholic Church is the only true church, far superior to all other churches. It knows all the answers and its holiness and righteousness know no limits.[98]

During the first thirteen or fourteen years after Vatican II, under the tentative and cautious leadership of Pope Paul VI (a very ascetic man who looked as though he carried the weight of the world on his shoulders) some efforts were made to recast the nature of the hierarchy. Support for a humble, collegial, participatory church, with the hierarchy sharing governance with laity, was widespread, as was the consensus that the time was right for the church to abandon its discredited medieval ways. There were attempts at shared decision making and a discussion of strategies to require accountability. Many forward thinking men were appointed to serve as bishops and cardinals.

In 1978, with the appointment of Karol Wojtyla, Cardinal of Cracow, Poland, as pope, the one step forward that had been taken by the church was followed quickly by two giant steps backwards. In the hierarchy, conservative members came to outnumber progressives. Cardinals and bishops again guarded the power and authority that they considered rightfully theirs; they imposed restraints on academic freedom and championed thought control; and they tended to rule with the same imperial manner and intimidation that had characterized the church in the Middle Ages. This pope and his subordinates seem to lead the church away from the path mapped out by Vatican II. On the one hand, they place enormous emphasis on the strong picture conveyed by a unified, centralized church that is clear on dogma, but, on the other hand, they have had difficulty dealing decisively with problems that are destroying the church, especially the sex abuse crisis.

Since revelations about hierarchical complicity by the reassignment of offending priests, the attitudes of Catholics have undergone a radical change. No longer are Catholics willing to allow their pastors to exercise unquestioned authority, nor are they susceptible to intimidation by bishops. Further, the fact that clerics are losing power does not disturb lay people; instead, they are distressed in knowing how hard bishops are fighting to hold on to authority, prestige and control. The present is a time of transition in which lay people are beginning to understand that they are entitled to answers and dependable stewardship from priests and bishops. Coverups, steps taken to silence the news media, attempts to dismiss instances of sexual molestation as isolated and not specific to the priesthood, and the overall holier-than-thou posture of prelates who cling tenaciously to their privileged positions are glaring problems with the Catholic Church. Compromising standards—even to the extent of abandoning them—in order to recruit seminarians, silencing critical and dissident voices, and the priority given to fiscal solvency over and above the church's spiritual mandate are other important issues that have come to light.

In the Bible we read accounts of how, in the first generations of Christianity, the church viewed itself as a community of believers in Jesus, bound to one another by the faith they shared and guided by God's hand. Bible stories recount how people who belonged to the church assisted each other in their needs, supported one another in their struggles, and had a clear sense of the meaning and purpose of life. There is no question that Catholics today yearn to belong to vital communities, to think of their church as "home," and of co-parishioners as "family." They crave spiritual fulfillment; they want to be less tense, less materialistic—more serene, more prayerful. People want to belong to church communities they can be proud of; they want their needs to be taken seriously and their gifts called forth for the good of all. They want to work for justice. They think that the hierarchy should be known for its integrity and responsiveness. While it would be hopelessly romantic to expect the church to be some kind of earthly utopia, Catholics do not think that they are asking too much when they request that the energy of church leaders be expended to sustain genuine religious communities.

Catholicism is supposed to be a sacrament, i. e., a visible sign of God's presence in a given place and at a particular time. The theory behind the notion of church as sacrament is that members of the church express their faith, hope, and charity in concrete ways, and through these acts Christ brings healing and salvation. People, then, experience God and are reminded of God's provident care when they encounter Christians who carry out Christ's works in ways that can be seen and felt. Individual intentional communities that organize themselves as churches, as well as the totality of these communities existing as the universal Catholic Church, are sacraments to the extent that their members resemble and make real their founder, Jesus Christ, in thought, prayer and deed. If Jesus returned today, would Jesus recognize today's church as the instrument destined to bring his message to the ends of the earth? What would he say to the pope, cardinals and bishops about their stewardship?

Perhaps it is unrealistic to expect an entity like the Catholic Church to render an unambiguous articulation of the message it is required to preach and to waste none of its energies on hypocritical speech. As it is, however, church leaders often choose words that are ambiguous, false, phony or defensive in order to paper over its freefall from credibility, and people strain their ears in vain hoping to catch a whisper of the message of Jesus. In light of the reality of the negligence of most bishops and the horrific misconduct of some priests, truth telling and righteous actions are desperately needed. The American bishops made a start in this direction at their June 2002 meeting in Dallas by adopting the Charter for the Protection of Children and Young People. Implementing the spirit and letter of the charter will require that they admit how they have been tarnished by clericalism, juridicism and triumphalism as well as their pledge to repent of these unholy attributes.

In the first days after Jesus' ascension, the nascent church was organized in various locations around bishops who unified communities and worked to strengthen these communities in their faith and connection to each other. Bishops were overseers whose own interests were secondary. The gospel of Jesus and the welfare of the people of God were primary. If, in those times, children were sexually molested, bishops probably did not look the other way but, rather, acted decisively to stop misconduct. The point of this hypothetical look backwards is to establish that there can be no question that the responsibility of bishops is to serve the interests of the church. Looking out for themselves or promoting a triumphalistic image of the church that is at odds with reality is theologically deceptive and ought not to be tolerated.

Theology of the Priesthood

The Catholic Church has beliefs about the priesthood and these beliefs constitute its "theology of the priesthood." People differ about theology of the priesthood. They argue that some aspects may be open to revision, or they contend that beliefs are unchangeable. The threshold issue concerns the nature of the priesthood. Has the essence of priesthood been set by divine determination, i. e., God's will, or by the New Testament, or by decisions of the early church, so that this essence cannot be changed?

Those who argue that the priesthood was established and fundamentally defined from the earliest days of the church believe that the apostles decided on how the church should be governed and that Jesus himself validated their authority. Since Jesus spoke as God, and directions for priesthood came from Jesus, the essence of Catholic priesthood represents the will of

God. Church leaders who reason along these lines state that the nature of the priesthood was set in ancient times and that this fact was established at the Council of Trent in the sixteenth century. Reaffirmed by Vatican II in the twentieth century, questions about priesthood have been settled and the answers should be accepted. The priesthood, according to Trent and Vatican II, is a cultic institution that men seek to join and in which ordained priests are set apart. Priests are to act as holy people who represent Jesus, as leaders and teachers of communities who alone can preside at the Eucharist, penance and the anointing of the sick. Bishops confer ordination on priests, creating a strong bond between bishop and priest; and priesthood, once conferred at ordination, can never be removed.

Those who see the nature of priesthood as open to modification tend to think that the priesthood is an institution that evolved within the culture of the ancient Near East. The way it took shape was affected by the needs and expectations of early Christians. Priesthood is a cult because it is derived from the order of Levi in the Old Testament. The Levites were one of the twelve tribes of Israel and the function of the Levites was to act as priests. In early Christianity, Jesus' followers gathered and broke bread in memory of him. Priesthood took form as the need to have presiders for the celebration of the Eucharist became apparent. Historians tell us that in the earliest times bishops presided at the Eucharist and eventually the office of priest was instituted. Bishops designated individuals to be priests when they themselves were not available to preside at Eucharists for the many communities that came into being. Scholars speculate that in Christianity there probably were no priests until after 95AD.[99]

Those who think of priesthood as open to modification question why there is such a pronounced separation of ordained from nonordained. When priesthood is thought of as unchangeable, the priest tends to be separated from the nonordained and the work of the priest is done without collaboration by the laity. A two-tiered system is instituted and lay people have lesser roles in the system than ordained people.

No matter how the priesthood is conceptualized, there is no dispute that celibacy is a matter of discipline. No one claims that celibacy represents the will of God or is a matter of fidelity to tradition or scripture. Celibacy was imposed on priests in the thirteenth century because the hierarchy judged that it would be better for the church to be served by celibate males than by married men. Since there is no question whatever that the hierarchy made this rule, overriding previous practice, there is no dispute that the hierarchy could make celibacy optional for priests, if it wished to do so, and return to earlier practice that allowed married priests.

At the present time priests who serve the church are ordained within a system that holds that priests are a separate group, set apart to exercise a sacred, cultic role. By virtue of this role they should strive for spiritual superiority, so as to resemble Jesus, the high priest. In addition to their sacramental ministry, priests are called to exercise the roles of prophet and shepherd. Up until the sex scandal broke they were considered "men of God." It would have been inconceivable to speak ill of them.

Evaluating the way priesthood is understood requires reconsideration of several aspects of priesthood and leads to significant questions. Should there be a distinct separation of priests from laity so that the roles and expectations of the laity are lesser than those of priests? Should the laity be called to greater spirituality, and to exercise prophetic and stewardship roles? As far as the discipline of the church is concerned, should there be optional celibacy? Those who consider priesthood open to modification want a discussion of the theology of priesthood so that a clarification of the nature of priesthood can occur; the uncritical appropriation of cultural aspects of ancient times, not the will of God, would then be revealed as the basis for much of what has become established.

The most significant aspect of the Catholic priesthood under debate is whether priests must be men or if women could also be ordained. Advocates for the ordination of women insist that just because there is no mention of women among the apostles in the New Testament does not mean that women cannot be priests. Because there are no accounts of women priests from the early church does not mean that there were not women priests, only that there is no acknowledged historical record of women presiding at the Eucharist. Additionally, advocates of women priests say that both men and women are meant to model Jesus and that male gender is not an absolute precondition for priesthood.

In spite of the fact that the issue of who can be a priest has been called into question, the thinking of John Paul II that women are not eligible, has not changed:

> Although the teaching that priestly ordination is to be reserved to men alone has been preserved by the constant and universal tradition of the Church and firmly taught by the Magisterium in its more recent documents, at the present time in some places it is nonetheless considered still open to debate, or the Church's judgment that women are not to be admitted to ordination is considered to have a merely disciplinary force.
>
> Wherefore, in order that all doubt may be removed regarding a matter of great importance, a matter which pertains to the

Church's divine constitution itself, in virtue of my ministry of confirming the brethren (cf. Lk 22:32) I declare that the Church has no authority whatsoever to confer priestly ordination on women and that this judgment is to be definitively held by all the Church's faithful.[100]

In the aftermath of the sex abuse crisis in the Catholic Church, questions about celibacy and the priesthood have come to the forefront. Is there a connection between the fact that priests have sexually molested minors and the fact that priests must commit to celibacy? Does the priesthood attract sexual criminals? Does the celibacy requirement result in more homosexual candidates than heterosexual candidates? If there is a disproportionate number of homosexuals, does this in some way provide an explanation for the large preponderance of cases of ephebophilia among the cases of sexual molestation of minors? Is there a rational explanation for why abusers have continued in ministry even though they would have been dismissed in any other line of work? Are lay people diminished because the superior spirituality of priests is assumed? Are lay people marginalized because meaningful ways of participating in the affairs of the church are limited to and controlled by priests and bishops? Let us consider these questions.

Celibacy, rightly practiced, requires a maturity and spirituality that would enable adherents to keep their vow. Celibate men testify that it is possible to live this way. But only a thorough empirical study of what priests actually feel and do would establish, or lay to rest, a connection between celibacy and molestation of minors. To date, no such study has taken place, though the need for it is unquestionable.[101]

In Article 17 of their recommendations for actions to be taken in dealing with sexual molestation, the bishops' committee declared:

> Given how pervasive the problem of the sexual abuse of children and young people is in our society, we offer to cooperate with other churches, institutions of learning and other interested organizations in conducting a major research study in this area.[102]

Unfortunately, by adopting this disingenuous stance and offering to conduct a collaborative study, the bishops do not appear to be willing to examine the reality of how the requirement of celibacy for Catholic priests might be related to the criminal compulsion of some priests, which results in the molestation of children. They also fail to find out how much of a hindrance the celibacy requirement is to men who feel called to work as priests but do not answer the call because of their unwillingness to make a lifelong commitment to sexual abstinence. These are exclusively Catholic questions, for which the bishops alone are in a position to obtain answers. In trying to dilute these questions, American bishops do not manifest the sincerity and openness necessary to look at the truth and get to the bottom of things.

Does the priesthood attract sexual criminals? The answer seems to be that those attracted to the priesthood are no more likely to commit sexual crimes than those attracted to other professions. The basis for this answer is that the number of sexual criminals among priests is less than two percent, not significantly different from the number in the general population.

Since the exodus from the American Catholic priesthood in the years after 1968, the composition of the priesthood has become more homosexual than heterosexual. Twenty thousand priests left, many of them to marry.[103] Without proper research into the sexual orientations of priests, accurate data about percentages is lacking. As far as homosexual priests and child molestation is concerned, it needs to be stated that gay men are no more likely to molest minors than are heterosexual men. The fact that ninety percent of sex abuse cases by priests involve boys may be attributable to the presence of more homosexuals than heterosexuals in the priesthood and may be an indication of this disparate proportion. Abuse of boys by priests may also reveal that many gay priests are fixated at an adolescent stage of sexual development. Psychologist and priest, Stephen J. Rossetti, President of St. Luke Institute, a treatment center for priest sex abusers, makes this point:

> ... a significant number of priests who sexually molest minors are involved with post-pubescent adolescent males, about 14 to 17 years of age. It appears to be true that many in this subpopulation of priest child-molesters are homosexually oriented. But theirs is a particular kind of homosexuality, which one might call "regressed" or "stunted." These homosexual men are emotionally stuck in adolescence themselves, and so are at risk for being sexually active with teenage males. The issue is therefore not so much homosexuality but rather their stunted emotional development.[104]

Ephebophilia entails sex between an adult man and an adolescent minor. During the meeting at the Vatican between American cardinals and officials of the curia in April 2002, the fact that most priest sexual misconduct involves ephebophilia rather than pedophilia was stressed. The purported explanation for ephebophilia was the fact that it is homosexual priests who act out this way. It was implied that homosexual priests who are guilty of ephebophilia do not take their vow of celibacy seriously and that perhaps homosexuals should not be priests.

Raising this point requires analyzing whether sexual intimacy between homosexual men and adolescents represents an aberrant practice or an acceptable practice for gay men. The law in most states makes the age of sixteen to eighteen the age of consent for a teenage girl. Law does not sanction sex involving same-sex partners and, in some states, same-sex acts are explicitly forbidden, so there is no comparable age of consent for gays. Mainstream spokespersons for homosexual rights endorse intimacy between adults and oppose relations between adults and minors. They object to the fact that Catholic cardinals associate ephebophilia with adult homosexual intimacy and claim that this is an invalid association. Dignity, USA, an organization for gay, lesbian, bisexual and transgendered Catholics, opposes making homosexual priests scapegoats for the negligence of the hierarchy. Marianne Duddy, a Dignity spokesperson, expressed outrage about "a witch hunt to oust gay priests" and said that efforts by the hierarchy to blame homosexual priests for the child molestation scandal is "a public relations exercise – one doomed to failure."[105]

Two issues regarding priests remain: the shortage of priests and the reason bishops reassigned sex offenders. The reasons why priest molesters have been reassigned seem to be pragmatic. Catholic priest and professor at John Carroll University, Donald B. Cozzens sees the fact of the priest shortage as the driving force. He writes,

> For most readers there is little need to review the staggering drop in the number of candidates studying for the priesthood in the theologates of North America and western Europe (c. 80 percent), nor the roughly 40 percent decline in the number of priests in these same geographical regions during the last three decades of the twentieth century. Some, however, may be unaware of the small number of priests under age forty. In the Diocese of Cleveland, for example, there were 240 priests age forty and under in 1970. In 1999 there were only 35. Researchers predict that by the year 2005, only one in eight priests will be under thirty-five, with the average age of priests close to sixty.[106]

Professor of history and religious studies at Penn State University, Philip Jenkins has some idea why bishops kept abusive priests in active ministry. There was a shortage of priests; in dioceses in the south and west of the United States, the shortage was so severe that priestless parishes were becoming common. Clergy and seminarians were such a "scarce commodity that bishops began to exercise wide latitude in regard to who was fit to be a priest" and local shortages of priests made it easy "to dispose of clergy who had encountered problems in one jurisdiction." In addition, the tracking of reassigned abusive priests became haphazard and bishops seemed unaware of the need to run a tight ship in their dioceses because the situation throughout the country was so lax.[107]

Questions of how lay people are limited by priests' superior and holier status prompt a look at the theology of the laity, the subject of our next section.

Theology of the Laity

Men and women Catholics who are not priests, religious sisters or brothers are known as the laity. Over the history of the church the status of the laity has changed. Before the emperor Constantine made Christianity the official religion of the Holy Roman Empire in the fourth century, lay people were actively involved with priests and bishops in the spiritual and administrative life of the church. Following Constantine, lines of demarcation were drawn, with the clergy assigned a higher classification than the laity. In the early church "the intervention of the laity was welcomed as a matter of principle."[108] After Constantine the laity learned that they were to occupy a lowly place. The sixteenth century Council of Trent hardened lines of delineation with the result that, from then until Vatican Council II, lay Catholics were instructed that they occupied the lowest rank in the church. In one respect what Vatican II attempted to accomplish was a return to the vision of Galatians, an understanding of the early church in which all divisions were destroyed "between Jew and gentile, male and female, slave and free." (Gal. 3:28)

Vatican II opened the status of the laity to reexamination, promoting a newfound respect. According to *Lumen Gentium,* one of the major documents issued at the Council,

The laity are gathered together in the People of God and make up the Body of Christ under one head. Whoever they are they are called upon, as living members, to expend all their energy for the growth of the Church and its continuous sanctification, since this very energy is a gift of the Creator and a blessing of the Redeemer.

The lay apostolate, however, is a participation in the salvific mission of the Church itself. Through their baptism and confirmation all are commissioned to that apostolate by the Lord Himself. Moreover, by the sacraments, especially holy Eucharist, that charity toward God and man which is the soul of the apostolate is communicated and nourished. Now the laity are called in a special way to make the Church present and operative in those places and circumstances where only through them can it become the salt of the earth. Thus every layman, in virtue of the very gifts bestowed upon him, is at the same time a witness and a living instrument of the mission of the Church itself "according to the measure of Christ's bestowal."

Besides this apostolate which certainly pertains to all Christians, the laity can also be called in various ways to a more direct form of cooperation in the apostolate of the Hierarchy. This was the way certain men and women assisted Paul the Apostle in the Gospel, laboring much in the Lord. Further, they have the capacity to assume from the Hierarchy certain ecclesiastical functions, which are to be performed for a spiritual purpose.

Upon all the laity, therefore, rests the noble duty of working to extend the divine plan of salvation to all men of each epoch and in every land. Consequently, may every opportunity be given them so that, according to their abilities and the needs of the times, they may zealously participate in the saving work of the Church.[109]

The faith of the church expressed in 1965 is that the laity is incorporated into Christ and is an essential part of the People of God. They share in the priestly, prophetic and kingly offices exercised by Jesus. The Catechism of the Catholic Church issued in 1994 explains how the laity exercises these offices. The lives of lay people include work and suffering and by their fidelity in enduring "all these they become spiritual sacrifices acceptable to God through Jesus Christ," thus, through their sacrifices, sharing in Jesus' priestly ministry.[110] As an aspect of sharing in Jesus' priesthood, the catechism recognizes the work of parents in raising their children: "In a very special way, parents share in the office of sanctifying 'by leading a conjugal life in the Christian spirit and by seeing to the Christian education of their children.'"[111]

Jesus exercised a prophetic role, and lay people share also in this ministry. The catechism says that lay people have both a right and a duty to make their opinions known. "In accord with the knowledge, competence, and preeminence which they possess, [lay people] have the right and even at times a duty to manifest to the sacred pastors their opinion on matters which pertain to the good of the Church, and they have a right to make their opinion known to the other Christian faithful, with due regard to the integrity of faith and morals and reverence toward their pastors, and with consideration for the common good and the dignity of persons."[112] Shaken from their complacence and angered by the betrayal of many of their bishops, Catholic men and women are beginning to stake claim to this prophetic role.

The primary reality of Jesus' kingly office is that Jesus rules as king in heaven. Being a monarch or king makes one the governor of a kingdom. Jesus rules over his Father's kingdom and the catechism tells us that lay men and women are expected to share in governance of the church. In the church, "lay members of the Christian faithful can cooperate in the exercise of this power [of governance] in accord with the norm of law." And so the church provides for their presence at particular councils, diocesan synods, pastoral councils; the exercise of the pastoral care of a parish, collaboration in finance committees, and participation in ecclesiastical tribunals, etc.[113] In theory, then, the right of lay men and women to cooperate in financial and legal aspects of administration of the church is clear. Translating theory into practice remains a daunting task.

That the hierarchy undermined parents' efforts to exercise their "priestly" functioning and returned priest molesters to ministry shows that the words bishops are supposed to live by do not always govern their actions.

When the hierarchy acknowledges that it is appropriate for church members to make their opinions known and then prevents organizations like Voice of the Faithful (VOTF) from finding a way of sharing governance, then the sincerity of church leaders needs to be questioned. Voice of the Faithful contends that "it is quite clear that mainstream Catholics want justice and support for the victims, support of good priests, bishop accountability for this scandal, and more lay involvement in the future in administrative issues of running the church. These concerns are represented by our current three main goals.

"VOTF believes that the laity needs to organize itself democratically. VOTF is NOT trying to make the church hierarchy democratic; we are simply talking about how the laity organize themselves. Laity organization and involvement is an important obligation and right under Canon Law and Vatican II and is not a radical idea."[114]

During the unfolding of the sex abuse crisis, cardinals and bishops frequently called for input and collaboration of lay people, but lay participation remains at the bishops' behest. There still is no mechanism for individuals or groups to gain recognition, or to force the hierarchy to listen to them. The hierarchy continues to select the individuals and groups with whom it interacts. While it is getting more difficult to ignore grassroots movements, the hierarchy still seems to be trying to do so.

Paragraph 911 of the catechism is a call to shared governance. Lay members should exercise pastoral care of parishes, collaboration in finance committees, and participation in ecclesiastical tribunals.[115] Bishop Wilton Gregory acknowledged the spirit of open participation when he said, "As we set about this task, we bishops are very conscious of the fact that we were not able to come to this moment alone, nor will be able to complete it alone. We realize, as perhaps never before, our corporate need for and this grace-filled opportunity of working more collaboratively with our devoted laity, religious and clergy."[116]

In order to implement shared governance, structures need to be designed for lay people to be involved in meaningful ways. Lay people need to know whom among them will be welcomed as collaborators, what they will be expected to do, where they should go, when they should appear, and why they should expect to be taken seriously. Without specifics, the words of Vatican II, the catechism, and the American bishops mean nothing.

As American bishops grapple with the issue of what the laity will be doing, they might want to consider some suggestions. In the early church there was a greater sense of community than there is today, with bishop-leaders being more connected to the faithful than is the case today. In fact, there are accounts of the faithful electing their bishops. Members of the American hierarchy might want to suggest the resumption of this process to authorities in Rome. If bishops served at the pleasure of those they lead, they would probably be more cognizant of the peoples' needs and more responsive of them.

There are good reasons to have parishioners interview candidates for pastor or associate pastor, to review their files, and to assure themselves that these individuals pose no danger and will likely serve communities appropriately.

Many lay people have expertise in finance, legal matters, child welfare and administration. These are secular functions for which lay people have been educated and in which they are competent. Discussions by bishops about handing over financial, legal and administrative functions to lay people should be undertaken with an openness on the part of the hierarchy to turning over work for which they are ill suited and which, in terms of the sex abuse crisis, they have performed miserably. In doing so, bishops could concentrate on the spiritual matters that are their primary responsibility.

Finally, bishops should consult scripture scholars, patristic scholars and historians to learn about the early church. A more informed hierarchy will acknowledge the wisdom of returning the church to its pre-Constantinian roots; surely, they will want to abandon the aberrations that became entrenched following the Council of Trent.

Listen

We are tempted, for example, to imagine this crisis is going to be swiftly and conclusively resolved by decisive action at this meeting (Dallas, June 2002). Decisive action is, of course, essential. It means that the church will not be in worse shape when you leave than when you arrived. But we know that even the best policy on paper must be implemented. We know that there remains a backlog of abuse cases to be addressed. We know that wounds have been opened, anger provoked, suspicions planted, and questions raised that cannot be dealt with here and now—but must be dealt with over time, conscientiously and purposefully.

What if we left here having really absorbed the idea that the Catholic Church in the United States will never be the same? We would know then that what is done here today and tomorrow can only be a down payment on what you—and what all of us—must do over years to come.

—Margaret O'Brien Steinfels[117]

Listening implies hearing what someone is saying. We remain at a dangerous crossroads. We stopped to consider what confronts the Catholic Church and we looked beneath the surface to consider what caused the crisis. We come now to our final task. It is time to listen and absorb what is being said. Who should listen? Certainly everyone who is interested in the recovery of the Catholic Church, the healing of victims, and the rule of law would benefit from listening. Specifically, however, it is the American Catholic hierarchy that has brought disgrace on the church. Cardinals and bishops are the people who need most to listen so that they can hear the suggestions that are being offered to assist the church to negotiate this crossroads. As much as the American hierarchy might wish to put the scandal behind them, they should not try to deceive themselves. Adopting the charter in Dallas in June and affirming the revised norms in Washington in November 2002 were giant steps in the right direction, but many voices are now raised to tell the hierarchy how to proceed. The bishops need to listen.

Listen to the Vatican

The bishops of the United States are under the authority of the pope in Rome; therefore, there is no question that bishops will listen to the pope and other Vatican officials.

When the bishops voted on June 14, 2002, to adopt the Charter for the Protection of Children and Young People, they knew that the charter they formulated could not become church policy in the Untied States until the Vatican approved it. As it turned out, authorities in Rome called for several changes in the charter and the bishops must do as Rome directs. What changes were instituted by the Vatican and how will these changes affect bishops' ability to deal decisively with child molestation by priests? Let us consider each of these questions in turn.

The Vatican asserted its ultimate authority by decreeing that all cases of priest molestation of minors should be reported to the Congregation for the Doctrine of the Faith and that American bishops should follow Vatican directions regarding how to proceed.[118] "Unless the Congregation for the Doctrine of the Faith, having been notified, calls the case to itself because of special circumstances, it will direct the diocesan bishop to proceed."[119] Thus, in handling cases of priest sexual abuse by church authorities, the Vatican will determine where the priest's church trial will be held. If it is not held in Rome, an accused priest will be tried in the United States by a church tribunal made up of priests who have been trained to carry out this work.[120] The thinking is that only the most sensational cases of priest sexual molestation involving large numbers of children will wind up in Vatican courts. And, it should be kept in mind that Vatican intervention and church proceedings represent a second type of trial for a priest accused of molestation; civil trials can go forward even as church intervention is underway.

The Vatican clearly expressed its intention that the reputations of accused priests be a priority as the church sets about examining charges against them. "All appropriate steps shall be taken to protect the reputation of the accused during the investigation."[121] While the Vatican prescribed that accused priests be temporarily removed from ministry, it left open the question of their guilt or innocence until the completion of a trial conducted by specially trained priests in accordance with Catholic canon law. As far as lay boards are concerned, the Vatican made the point that these boards are advisory in nature and that it is bishops who have the final say about decisions. Further, the Vatican required that members of advisory boards be Catholics in good standing, and it eliminated appellate boards that were intended to handle appeals of decisions. The Vatican held that its statute of limitations be in effect in church trials. This statute expires after an abuse victim turns twenty-eight years old but, in the face of credible accusations, bishops may ask the Vatican for exemptions allowing them to ban priests from ministry even if the statute has expired.[122] In a sense, the American bishops had no choice but to accept the Vatican revisions and they did so by a vote of 246 to 7 with 6 abstentions. On December 16, 2002, these revised rules were made official church law by the Vatican.

How will the Vatican's changes affect bishops' ability to deal decisively with the scourge of clergy sex abuse? This is a difficult question to answer because the bishops adopted a charter in June that they had only just begun to implement before the Vatican imposed significant changes. The parties with competing interests in this process are the Vatican, American bishops, sex abuse victims, lawyers for the church, and lawyers for the victims, the media, and Catholic lay people. In Dallas in June, reeling from bad news that had bombarded them on a daily basis for more than five months, the American bishops crafted their response with the voices of victims, victims' lawyers, media critics and angered lay people echoing in their ears. Since the Vatican and church lawyers knew that this was the case, Rome reasserted the upper hand in the revised document by insisting on safeguarding the rights of accused priests and redefining the role of the laity so as to correct any mistaken impression about the laity's merely advisory role. Vatican authorities made themselves the final arbiter of an accused priest's fate.

That Vatican authorities can dictate to bishops in the United States how to carry out their duties as leaders of the church is not in question. However, the Vatican does not decide whether or not American bishops act with courage and integrity. And no policy statement can facilitate or prevent the exercise of these essential traits. Hence, although the Vatican has somewhat restricted the ability of bishops in the United States to take charge of sex abuse cases, the Vatican has not prevented American bishops from keeping men credibly charged with molesting minors from ministering as priests.

Bishops have to abide by the revised norms and the revised norms are weaker than the original norms. The original norms cared more about harm to children than the reputations of priests who are accused of child molestation. And the original norms gave lay people power to exercise an important oversight function. If the bishops were looking for loopholes, they probably could have found them in the June charter. It may be easier to locate loopholes using the norms ratified in November 2002. The bottom line, therefore, is that bishops need to abide by their consciences as well as the echo of a crying twelve year old boy who cannot sleep because he cannot purge his mind of the memory of a priest's raping him in a sacristy as he was finishing up his altar boy tasks.

Listen to critics

During their historic meeting in Dallas, Bishop Wilton Gregory acknowledged that some of the media coverage of the church crisis was constructive. "We bishops accept the challenge of this insightful coverage to do a better job in the fulfillment of our responsibilities."[123] Bishop Gregory, as most of his confreres, objected to salacious and sensationalistic aspects of media reporting, but he did well to make a distinction and affirm the challenge contained in thoughtful analysis coming from individuals in the church and the media. The bishops, and all interested parties, would do well to listen to and act upon this analysis.

A fundamental flaw in the hierarchy's approach to the sex abuse crisis is that the focus has been placed almost exclusively on how to deal with accusations and what to do about priests who are rightly or wrongly accused. There is no question that this is an extremely critical component of response but the absence of attention to causes of the problem represents a serious omission. The threshold question that cries out for an answer is: *Why did this happen?* This should be item one on the hierarchy's agenda. In this regard, Donald B. Cozzens, a priest who teaches at John Carroll University, offers an informed opinion.

As vicar (of the diocese of Cleveland), I met annually with chancellors and vicars from across the United States. ...Underneath the scrambling efforts of bishops and vicars to respond effectively and pastorally to the crisis, questions about the meaning and implications of the violating behaviors were studiously avoided. We became absorbed with the task at hand: how to handle the present crisis, *this crisis.* I recall no thoughtful discussion about the causes of the problem, its meaning or implications. Attempts to do so were often met with a certain suspicion that a particular agenda was at work. ...no serious investigation has been launched into the origin of clergy sexual misconduct with minors...[124]

Examination of the crisis reveals that there are greater and lesser problems. Yes, victims scarred for life because of a priest's crime represent the most horrific and visible sign that something truly dreadful happened. But, in trying to come to terms with the problem of priest misconduct, something even more disturbing than its existence may be the way the church structures and governs itself. In spite of what the catechism and Vatican II say, cardinals and bishops do not share governance and expend enormous effort to control the flow of information. Prophets function in the Judeo-Christian tradition to point out systemic injustice and call those who act unjustly to account. Professor Scott Appleby took on the role of prophet when he addressed the bishops in Dallas:

> What are they saying about you?...They are saying...that this scandal is only incidentally about the...sexual abuse of minors by a small minority of priests....The underlying scandal is the behavior and attitudes of the Catholic bishops....They are saying, most distressingly, that the seminaries and the priesthood have been made vulnerable to the unstable and to the immoral...They are saying...that the Church...is morally bankrupt...They are saying that the failures of the hierarchy extend to your arrogation of unchecked authority over finances and legal strategies, extending to cover-ups and fiscal malfeasance. On this matter of reassigning predator priests, the apologies issuing from bishops and cardinals will not be heard unless and until they go beyond the rhetoric of "mistakes and errors" and name the protection of abusive priests for what it is—a sin, born of the arrogance of power.... A remark-

able...and...encouraging development...is the fact that Catholics on the right, and the left, and in the "deep middle" all are in basic agreement as to the causes of this scandal: a betrayal of fidelity enabled by the arrogance that comes with unchecked power.[125]

The American Catholic Church has the ability to raise huge amounts of money, more than seven billion dollars annually, making it comparable to a large corporation. Cozzens says that the temptation to respond as a corporation, to put concern for diocesan assets and the church's image before pastoral issues, has happened in the past.[126] Bishops mandate that a percentage of the money that goes into the basket be forwarded to the diocese and they have annual campaigns to add more funds to their treasuries. They do not have to provide many answers regarding how much money they administer or how funds are allocated. This makes possible a wide array of unorthodox practices, secret deals and fiscal irregularities. If bishops did not hold so much discretionary power, they would not have been able to make financial settlements with abuse victims and suppress disclosure of what transpired between abuser and victim. Police would have been called more frequently and the American justice system would have dealt with priests who were found guilty of sexual molestation. Money kept the police and the courts at bay, money about which Catholics know little. In this regard, *Business Week* Boston correspondent William C. Symonds writes:

> ...many of the doors that could reveal a true picture of the Church's finances remain tightly sealed. Kenneth Korotky, chief financial officer of the USCCB, says the U.S. Church has not even attempted to prepare a consolidated financial statement. Although Chicago, Detroit, Shreveport, and other dioceses do disclose their numbers, some of the largest—including New York and Philadelphia—refuse to release financial reports....Charles E. Zech, an economics professor at Villanova University,...says 38% of Catholics don't know how parish donations are being spent. The same secrecy has obscured just how much the Church has paid out so far in settlements and how much more could be on the line.[127]

In addition to money individuals give to the church, it receives considerable funding from wealthy foundations. FADICA, an acronym for Foundations and Donors Interested in Catholic Activities, is an organization that represents fifty wealthy Catholic donors that contribute approximately two hundred million dollars a year to the church in the United States.

Alarmed by the sex abuse scandal and distressed that money contributed in good faith for constructive purposes might be going to finance secret payoffs, FADICA, through its president Frank J. Butler, asked the bishops for an accounting. What FADICA wanted the bishops to undertake was to have the conference "hire an outside auditor to survey the money paid by the nation's 194 dioceses over two decades for abuse settlements, lawyers' fees and other costs resulting from sexual misconduct by clergymen."[128]

With the exception of disclosures from Baltimore, Chicago and Belleville, Illinois, FADICA's request fell on deaf ears. The bishops did not even put it on the agenda for their November meeting. When the question was raised as to why FADICA's request was being treated dismissively, a bureaucratic response was offered about how each diocese operated independently, so that there is no central office that can compel compliance. Kenneth Korotky, the chief financial officer of the United States Conference of Catholic bishops, said, "Each diocese stands alone, and we cannot promulgate rules on financial accountability," but added that recently there has been a trend toward more openness.[129]

It is clear that the bishops need to listen to wealthy donors like Erica John of Milwaukee, an heiress to the

Miller brewing fortune.

> We are the church, and the leaders to whom
> we entrust our religious patrimony are failing
> us. We as funders think it's important that
> the bishops open their books and come clean,
> because some of us are beginning to feel dis-
> appointed and even alienated from the
> church.[130]

In a Gallop poll, commissioned by FADICA, twenty percent of Catholics said that they had stopped
donating to their diocese, one in nine regular church-
goers said they had been putting less than usual in the
basket and only three percent of Catholics, mostly
more affluent and conservative parishioners, reported
increases in their parish giving.[131]

Because American bishops have succeeded in
bypassing the legal system they have been able to neglect the moral requirement that they act as responsible
citizens. Criminal priests were not prosecuted and
removed from society. From this the perception has
taken hold that bishops have been grossly negligent.
Although he is generally supportive of the way bishops
have handled the crisis, Stephen J. Rossetti, the priest-
psychologist who is president of a treatment center for
priests charged with sexual molestation of minors, crit-

icizes gag orders. "The diocese agrees to settle a civil suit; it pays out a certain sum of money, and it stipulates that the victim will not publicly reveal what happened. In retrospect, this can be recognized as a mistake. While one can understand a bishop's desire not to 'scandalize' people and to protect the church's image, such actions promote distrust and allegations of secrecy."[132]

Beginning in 2002, relentless publicity made it impossible for the hierarchy to maintain the upper hand in damage control. No longer were they able to achieve respectability though the intervention of public relations experts. Neither were the bishops successful in silencing their opponents. During the 1984 Gauthe case in Louisiana, Jason Berry wrote that a wealthy Catholic, Edmund Reggie and his longtime friend Monsignor Alexander Sigur had asked the board chairman of a hospital to threaten to pull an advertising account from the *Times of Acadiana* to neutralize the paper's coverage of Gauthe's misconduct. A car dealership had already canceled and it was apparent that threatened boycotts chilled the publisher's veins.[133] Pressure tactics, exercised by their allies, worked to the advantage of the Catholic bishops, at least temporarily, but in the long run they undermined forthright and decisive action aimed solely at protecting minors.

As this crisis has played out over almost twenty years, bishops should have learned the lesson that suppression of free speech is a bad idea but, in this regard, they seem to be slow learners. Two examples from their meeting in Dallas support this contention. Representatives of the victim group SNAP (Survivors' Network of those Abused by Priests) were told by Bishop Gregory that they could not speak in Dallas because they filed a class action lawsuit to void secrecy provisions of settlements.[134] More interested in communicating with the bishops than in pursuing legal action, SNAP withdrew from the suit and their members were then rescheduled to speak. David Clohessy, director of the group, wrote, "We don't want anything to get in the way of genuine dialogue that might ultimately benefit children. That's why ... we are withdrawing from the suit."[135] Given the bishops' pledge to openness, Gregory's tactics with SNAP do not make sense.

As it turned out, Bishop Gregory and the American bishops did an about face and allowed three victims to speak about the abuse they endured and how they suffered psychologically and physically as a result.[136] Their testimony was riveting and media coverage of it was extensive. If anyone in the public at large were ignorant of what happened to victims or lacked understanding of how horrific sexual abuse is, victim accounts served to make members of the public knowledgeable and aware. In a sense, victims upstaged bishops and the usual discussions and administrative technicalities that ordinarily occupy the bishops' conference were eclipsed by dramatic stories of how children were molested by priests.

In another example of the bishops' refusal to be open to scrutiny in Dallas, they did not allow reporters from the *Boston Globe*, the newspaper that broke the Geoghan story and stayed with it in relentless fashion, to have press credentials. The bishops argued that the newspaper broke a story about a draft of their policy before the embargo was lifted. The *Globe* viewed the bishops' motivation differently: "The bishops' conference singled out the *Globe* for punishment solely because we did our job as journalists," said *Globe* editor Martin Baron. "We obtained a copy of the bishops' draft policy on sex abuse from an independent source and we published the contents before the bishops formally announced it. In an act of recrimination, the bishops have excluded the *Globe* from the floor of the conference. This sort of behavior is surprising and disappointing, and we can only hope it does not continue."[137] Perhaps under ordinary circumstances the bishops' decision could be supported, but these are not ordinary times. Continuing to control who will speak and who will have access to a story cannot be defended.

The bishops of the United States meet twice a year, in June and in November. When the bishops met in November 2002 in Washington, D. C., their meeting once again had the flavor of business as usual. Victims of priest abuse were not scheduled to speak; there were no dialogue sessions at which bishops could brief victims or vice versa. On the agenda were internal church matters, a resolution urging caution on going to war in Iraq, and approval of the norms revised by the Vatican that govern dealing with priests who are accused of molesting minors. There was no question that the bishops at this meeting were simply rubber-stamping this Vatican vetted document.

"The victims who were in evidence in June," wrote Michael Paulson and Michael Rezendes in the *Boston Globe*, "were conspicuous by their absence and had even been pushed out of the way by being prohibited from gathering in the lobby of the hotel at which the conference was being held. Unlike in Dallas, when the bishops allowed victims and selected lay intellectuals to address them, at this meeting there is no plan for any discussion between bishops and victims or lay leaders."[138]

Susan Troy, a leader in the Voice of the Faithful movement, said she was puzzled by Bishop Gregory's speech to the conference where he exhorted his fellow bishops to accept assistance from the laity, while many bishops refuse to talk with Voice of the Faithful members. "He said he needs us and that the bishops need us, but we're here and we don't think we're part of the discussion," Troy said.[139] Obviously, the bishops at their November meeting showed a decided inability to listen;

under the circumstances, this was an incredible omission.

Listen to VOTF and other organizations
After what transpired in 2002 concerning the sexual abuse of minors by Catholic priests, the point that bishops need to listen to interested lay people should not have to be stated; it should be self evident. However, this is not the case. How can this be? The answer lies in the nature of hierarchical self-understanding. The Catholic hierarchy, for the most part, is characterized by strong conservative tendencies. Bishops and cardinals believe that they are in charge of the church and that it is their job to preserve tradition. They consider themselves superior people with a clearly defined job description and they decide what is open to discussion and to whom they will listen. They authorize the formation of groups, giving organizations legitimacy or denying legitimacy, a slow and tedious process. In addition to their responsibility for keeping Catholic doctrine intact, bishops raise, appropriate, and spend money. They make all major administrative decisions in the Catholic Church. For hundreds of years, or as long as anyone can remember, this has been the reality. Bishops have the last word and can listen to advisors, or not, as they choose.

The status quo is a strong reality and the conservative status quo operative in the Catholic hierarchy tends to remain intransigent against changes not proposed by bishops themselves. Within this context the Catholic sex abuse scandal of 2002 occurred along with the emergence of an organization of vocal, demanding lay people in Boston.

In the beginning, in February 2002, in a church basement, a few dozen people met to talk about the scandal erupting around them. They evolved into a group that called for change in the church so that egregious administrative negligence would cease.

Early on Cardinal Law and his assistants did not pay much attention to VOTF, probably thinking that the movement would run out of steam. The media, however, was interested in the group and gave it publicity. In addition, leaders of the group were electronically savvy and used email and the Internet to promote their message. As winter yielded to spring and then to summer and beyond, VOTF continued to attract members so that by December 2002 there were 25,000 members throughout the world and VOTF chapters in forty U.S. states.

In view of what was happening, one might think that members of the hierarchy would be inclined to dialogue with groups like VOTF, learning from them what steps could be taken to restore the credibility of the church. That has not been the case. Even Bishop Wilton Gregory, who gained admiration for his openness and willingness to listen to people in Dallas, began to change his tune at the November meeting. Addressing the conference of bishops in Washington, Gregory said, "Sadly, even among the baptized there are those at extremes within the church who have chosen to exploit the vulnerability of the bishops in this moment to advance their own agendas. One cannot fail to hear in the distance – and sometimes very nearby, the call of the false prophet. 'Let us strike the shepherd and scatter the flock.'"[140] While Gregory did not directly refer to VOTF as a divisive force, there was no question that that organization was a target of his ire.

Nine dioceses banned VOTF from using church facilities for their meetings. In the archdiocese of Newark, concerned that some lay people might come forward and request permission to meet in a Catholic parish, Archbishop John J. Myers actually took the preemptive step of banning the group in advance.[141] The bishops refused to acknowledge the legitimacy of VOTF for such reasons as the group's vague mission statement, as well as the charge that VOTF is a clandestine cover for dissent, harboring people who want to change church doctrine.[142] Since the bishop is the guardian of Catholic doctrine, bishops claim that they cannot yield authority to groups like VOTF. In so doing, bishops overlook the fact that the slogan of VOTF is "Keep the faith, change the church," and that organization leaders have repeatedly stated that they accept church doctrine but object to management practices of bishops.

VOTF leaders reject the way bishops describe them and object to the way many in the hierarchy treat them. They say that they are practicing Catholics who love their faith but who cannot overlook or countenance the mismanagement of bishops. In the midst of the ongoing scandal, VOTF members were astounded that the bishops have taken the trouble to maintain a concerted effort to discredit them. Group members state again and again that they do not want to change doctrine but only to change church structures so as to prevent children from ever again being sexually molested by priests.

Before he resigned as archbishop, Cardinal Law actually did an about face as collections went down and criticism of him intensified. On November 26, 2002, he attended a meeting with four leaders of VOTF. The cardinal told group members that they should have asked his permission before forming and told them that lay people advise him through pastoral councils. Group leaders asserted their right as adult baptized Catholics to join together and formulate positions. Further, they questioned the ability of groups such as pastoral councils to be really independent in view of the fact that members are appointed by bishops.[143]

While VOTF did not get any concessions from Law at the meeting, the fact that they met with him represented a significant concession. In view of the many statements made by Catholic bishops in 2002 about collaborating with the laity, it is difficult to believe that a leader of the Catholic Church would make news just by attending a meeting.

If there is an urgent new truth emerging from the clergy sex abuse scandal, it is that bishops should not stall about negotiating with members of VOTF and other lay groups or try to undermine the existence of these groups. Bishops have to hear what people are thinking about administrative and financial accountability and have to be willing to put priest personnel files on the table for examination by lay leaders. After all, as New Jersey VOTF member Theresa Padovano said, "Whose parish is it? Whose money built those facilities?...Why don't they just talk to us? They have nothing to fear from us."[144]

Listen to VOTO

As the sex abuse scandal plays out, those directly affected by it, such as Catholic priests in good standing, find several reasons to be concerned. Accordingly, the Boston Priests Forum was organized to discuss matters of concern and in September 2002, VOTO, which stand for Voice of the Ordained, was established in New York City to consider how priests can protect their interests. VOTO differs from the Boston group in that it goes across diocesan lines and is open to any priest who wants to join.

In general, priests' groups as well as individual priests are concerned about how the new church policies will affect them. There was worry that the Dallas policy denied due process, defined sexual abuse too broadly, and imposed the same harsh punishment no matter what the degree of misconduct.[145] While the Vatican intervention that resulted in the revised norms took account of some of these issues, moving in the direction of satisfying priests, priests have raised other matters that need to be addressed.

"We want to show that within canon law, priests and the laity and religious have a right to be heard and to speak up, a right that this present administration in church and the present Vatican has taken away," said Father James E. Sullivan.[146] No one can argue with Sullivan, but his comment indicates the minefield in which bishops and priests tackle today's crisis. What was once a culture of silence regarding victims and potential child victims has evolved into a culture dismissive of the rights of priests. For this reason, priests are raising the alarm.

Canon lawyer Monsignor William A. Varvaro advised priests not to admit any sexual abuses to their bishops, who under the current policies must report all violations to the authorities and permanently remove the man from ministry.[147] While there is likely to be no public support for Varvaro's advice from the hierarchy and absolute rejection of it by lay Catholics, this advice represents but one end of the spectrum. At the other end are more reasonable complaints about policy. Priests request that those who have only been accused of sexual molestation but not convicted not be publicly named as they have a right to be considered innocent until proven guilty. Additionally, by not disclosing the name of a man who is falsely accused, authorities will not find themselves in the awkward position of later trying to restore the priest's reputation, an impossible task. Illustrating how this scandal has gone full circle, VOTO is now discussing how priests can bring charges against bishops who violate their rights.[148]

There is undeniable tension between the interests of priest groups and the agenda of lay and victim groups. This tension needs to be resolved without harming either side. The major chord heard since the revelations in Boston in January 2002 should not be drowned out. Molesters must go and structures that allow molesters to have access to children must be changed. That said, the minor chord that concerned priests are playing is that falsely accused priests should not be persecuted. This is completely reasonable and needs to be heard. It is a matter of justice to guard against a climate in which false charges flourish. If a falsely accused priest is exonerated, he needs to be fully restored to the ministry with appropriate steps taken to restore his reputation to the extent that this is possible.

Priest groups are correct in demanding due process. But is the zero tolerance policy that removes a priest permanently from ministry following a single credible charge of molestation past or present reasonable, or too harsh? Since Catholicism is a religion of repentance and forgiveness, if a priest has only a single charge against him, has completed a program of therapy, and subsequently does not harm children, should he be allowed to return to restricted ministry under supervision?

The argument in favor of allowing restricted ministry is that it seems humane and reasonable to give a priest a second chance, especially if the "abuse" was not horrific. The argument against allowing the priest to continue in ministry is that the only person who is going to abuse a second child is someone who already abused a first victim and that in the past supervision did not work. No pastor can watch an assistant pastor round the clock, thus leaving the door open to repeated misconduct.

Considering these arguments leads to acknowledgement of the importance of defining sexual abuse precisely. There are people who say that a priest who shared a dirty joke with a teenager or smacked a boy on the backside could be charged with abuse and his lifework ended. Of course, this would be over-reactive. However, to dismiss other forms of misconduct as less than criminal is unjustifiable. Therefore, a balance needs to be reached that safeguards the rights of all.

There are close to 46,000 priests in the United States; 30,000 of them are diocesan priests who are under the supervision of the bishop of a diocese. The other 15,000 are members of religious orders. These men are under the authority of a superior who reports to the pope. Superiors of religious orders belong to an organization called the Major Superiors of Religious Men. These superiors met in July 2002 in Philadelphia to consider how they would deal with religious order priests who abused children. Their response was different from that of the bishops, who are going to prohibit priests who molested children from wearing clerical garb or carrying out any assignments as priests. In other words, the bishops are going to shut down the ministry of priests who are guilty of sex abuse.

The major superiors, on the other hand, see their responsibility to their members differently. They think that "the lifelong vows of poverty, chastity and obedience that commit the priests, monks and brothers to their Catholic communities obligate their religious superiors to support them financially and to oversee them throughout their lives, even if they commit sexual crimes."[149] The superiors understand that they need to supervise members who have abused children and restrict these priests' or brothers' movements so that they do not come into contact with minors, but this is what they see themselves as bound by their vows to do. Residing as they do in communities with many members in the same place, their policy has the advantage that established structures exist for supervising religious men charged with sexual abuse of minors.

When the statute of limitations has expired and no criminal charges can be brought, a priest, either a diocesan priest or a religious order priest, is beyond the reach of the law and thus he cannot be prosecuted and incarcerated. If diocesan bishops get rid of these men, they will no longer be priests and will reside anonymously in residential communities. No one will be aware of the danger they pose. Religious order priests who abused children and who are beyond the law's reach will be supervised. This is obviously a better situation for public safety.

Listen to Scripture

The Bible is a collection of literature, composed of 73 books. Though the old and new testaments contain the Word of God, it would be a mistake to look to the Bible for explicit directions about what to do to deal with current problems. The Bible provides general wisdom and guidelines that are instructive but these need to be altered to fit particular circumstances.

We read in the gospel of Matthew: "And Jesus called

a child to Himself and set him before them, and said, 'Truly I say to you, unless you are converted and become like children, you shall not enter the kingdom of heaven. Whoever then humbles himself as this child, he is the greatest in the kingdom of heaven. And whoever receives one such child in my name receives me; but whoever causes one of these little ones who believe in me to stumble, it is better for him that a heavy millstone be hung around his neck, and that he be drowned in the depth of the sea. What terrible things will come on the world through scandal.'"(Matthew 18:2-7) From this passage it is apparent that children are esteemed for their innocence and that leading children astray is absolutely and totally against Jesus' teaching.

The Old Testament teaches that justice should be done to the vulnerable. "I will draw near to you for judgment against...those who defraud widows and orphans." (Malachi 3:5) And "learn to do good. Make justice your aim: redress the wrong, hear the orphan's plea." (Isaiah 1:17) Orphans were the most vulnerable persons in ancient Jewish society because they lacked a parent or parents to care for them. Being attentive to the needs of orphans and not defrauding them were basic requirements of those who followed the God of Abraham. By extension we can reason that in contemporary society children should be respectfully treated, whether they are orphans, children with a single parent or children who have two parents. Had a biblical author specifically addressed sexual molestation of a child, the author would have condemned this crime in the strongest of terms.

The notion that whatever you did to the least of the brothers and sisters of Jesus would count as being done to him is communicated in the parable about the last judgment in Matthew 25:31-46. Children are not a category in this parable, but they easily could be. Allowing one's spiritual imagination to envision this possibility conjures up a vision of the horror of an adult abusing a child and Jesus saying, "If you did it to the least of my brothers or sisters, you did it to me." This digression provides motivation to make whatever changes are necessary to end forever the possibility of children being abused by priests.

In extrapolating from these scriptural passages we can conclude that there is a basic requirement binding on all members of the Christian community to respect the innate dignity of each child. Decency and common humanity require that no one use superior status to exploit vulnerable persons. The simplicity and single heartedness of children that are affirmed in the gospels must be upheld. The horror and outrage of destroying a young person's innocence are revealed by the Bible.

Listen to victims
As hard and painful as it is for bishops to listen to

accounts of what was done to victims of sexual abuse and how their lives have been affected in the aftermath, it needs to continue. After cardinals met with victims in Dallas and the entire conference listened to speeches from three victim-survivors, a reporter spoke to Cardinal Anthony Bevilacqua. "Although the sexual abuse crisis has been shaking the church for 17 years, Cardinal Bevilacqua said it was the first time he had met a victim face to face. He described the experience as 'very emotional.' "[150] Bevilacqua went on to say, "A number of them expressed the sufferings they endured, the actual experiences. I had read much about these victims and I had to be honest with them and tell them that I try in every way to feel their pain, and listen to them and try to help them in every way possible."[151] Cardinals and bishops must get beyond consultations among themselves and with legal and public relations advisors and listen to victims of sexual abuse. They need to have first hand contact with men and women, boys and girls who have been violated so that they will never again deal with instances of this crime in a detached manner, at arms length from reality.

Listen to the laity

The bishops' meetings to deal with the sex abuse scandals are over. Bishops have registered their remarks about lay collaboration. But they are far from finished in this regard. It would be wrong for the bishops to now return to business as usual. Beyond consultation and collaboration with groups like VOTF, bishops need to be in touch with laity so as to learn how they want to be involved in governing the church. Once all areas of collaboration are determined, the hierarchy must move from the planning phase to the action phase.

Panels at the diocesan level that are charged to review allegations of priest sexual misconduct and make recommendations to the bishop must be independent and their decisions must be implemented. In spite of Vatican back stepping, if bishops reject the recommendations of lay panels that call for barring specific priests from future ministry, all efforts expended to correct abuses will have been in vain. Under no circumstances should the independence of lay advisory panels be compromised. Since the people who serve on these panels represent the conscience of both the church and the community, there must be nothing preventing them from exercising prudent oversight. Bishops should listen to these boards and follow their directives.

Listen to the Keating Commission and the Director of the Office for Child and Youth Protection

On June 14, 2002, Governor Frank Keating of Oklahoma was appointed by Bishop Wilton Gregory to chair a special lay commission that will ensure that the policies stated in the Charter for the Protection of Children and Young People are carried out. Keating said, "Many leaders of my church have a great deal to be guilty about these days, and *mea culpas* are not enough. The public, and especially the Catholic laity, will watch what they say, but we will also watch what they do to right past wrongs and to protect the vulnerable and the innocent. The commission will insist that action follows word, that deeds are consistent with the stated intent of the charter."[152]

On July 25, 2002 the names of those selected by the bishops to serve with Governor Keating were announced. In addition to Keating there are twelve distinguished Catholic lay people, four women and eight men from all parts of the United States, with a broad range of professional competencies.[153] Victim groups complained that the only victim-survivor on the panel was Michael Bland, an employee of the archdiocese of Chicago rather than a person unaffiliated with the Catholic Church.[154] In addition, reservations were lodged against one other member, a psychiatrist who disagrees with the legitimacy of the phenomenon of recovered or repressed memories. Paul R. McHugh, a former chair of the department of psychiatry and behavioral sciences at Johns Hopkins University School of Medicine, survived criticism of his appointment, and continues as a member of the board.[155]

It remains to be seen how effectively the Keating commission and the hierarchy will work together. In remarks, Governor Keating suggested that "withholding contributions and changing churches were the only real leverage lay people had to persuade church leaders to comply with the policy."[156] In a speech at Regis College in Boston, Keating slammed *The Pilot,* the Boston archdiocesan newspaper, for what he described as a "gratuitous assault" on his service to the church. *The Pilot* accused Keating of encouraging Catholics to commit mortal sin when he suggested that Catholics unhappy with their bishops consider worshiping in another diocese.[157] The fact that Catholic hierarchy and laity have entered a new era and that the church needs to be reformed requires that the bishops take heed of what the governor and his colleagues say and that they reject attempts to discredit the commission.

Keating and his associates plan to investigate episcopal neglect and to make recommendations to reform church structures. In doing this they will need to be forthright and uncompromising and the bishops will need to heed the recommendations they receive.

As the work of this national commission goes forward people all around the world will be curious to learn the result. Will the bishops listen, or will the bishops balk at being on the receiving end of directions that they do not like? Wisdom dictates that the bishops should listen to the governor and his panel and do as they are told. This reversal of roles is necessary.

In complying with their own charter, on November 7, 2002, the American bishops appointed Kathleen L. McChesney, a former F.B.I. agent to oversee their compliance with the sexual abuse policy. To this end, the bishops established a new office responsible for monitoring how well the bishops comply with their own norms.[158] McChesney's selection was hailed by leaders of victim's groups who were relieved that she appears to be independent of the bishops and has considerable investigative experience.[159] Janet Patterson, leader of a chapter of SNAP said, "It is important that the individual who looks at abuse cases for this commission be an independent professional with experience in investigating crime and a healthy degree of skepticism toward those who have concealed crimes."[160]

Given that neither the Keating Commission nor Kathleen McChesney has the power to authorize the removal from office of derelict bishops, it is crucially important that both reserve to themselves the power to communicate malfeasance to both the Vatican and the American public so that members of the hierarchy and superiors of religious men who do not comply with the policies they have agreed to are exposed for their misdeeds and driven from office by unrelenting public outcry.

Listen in a new way

Bishops are accomplished at listening to those above them in the chain of command. Now the bishops need to cultivate a new manner of listening. The people under them now need to be heard. In the past, bishops developed a facility for ignoring, sidestepping and punishing those who rank beneath them. In the wake of this scandal it is obvious that their way of relating to lay people needs to change. Just as they are beginning to comprehend the importance of really listening to victim-survivors, the bishops need to become responsive to what the laity and people in the broader society are saying. They also need to hear the anguish in the voices of demoralized clergy. Listening to and working with consultants they hire, or delegating responsibility for listening to victim stories to their associates, is no longer acceptable. In the past the victims were silenced, the laity was in the dark, and cardinals and bishops claimed that they were too busy to deal hands-on with personnel matters. This cannot continue. New times call for new dynamics and a new hierarchical listening style. American cardinals and bishops who ignore this call to listen do so at their peril.

Conclusion

It is important to understand that the Catholic Church in the United States hit bottom in 2002. What we have considered in these pages is the ugly reality of a dysfunctional institution corrupted by the arrogant complicity of the hierarchy in the disgusting sins of a relatively small number of child molesting priests. Since things could not have been worse for the church, and since its leaders could no longer postpone coping with this tragic reality, they have been forced by circumstances to begin the recovery process. Some important first steps have been taken. Much remains to be done. As we finish our overview of what went wrong it would not hurt to hear an encouraging word from the God whom believers hear in the scriptures: "Know that I am with you always until the end of the world."(Matthew 28:20)

Endnotes

1 Remarks by Arthur Austin regarding Fr. Paul Shanley and the Archdiocese of Boston, Survivors Network website, http://www.survivorsnetwork.org/

2 David E. Sanger, "NATO Gives Russia A Formal Welcome," *The New York Times,* May 29, 2002, A12

3 Margaret O'Brien Steinfels, "The Present Crisis through the Lens of the Laity," USCCB, June 13, 2002, 3

4 Philip Jenkins, *Pedophiles and Priests, NY: Oxford University Press, 1996, 81*

5 Stephen J. Rossetti, "The Catholic Church and Child Sexual Abuse," *America,* April 22, 2002, 10

6 ibid.

7 Sam Dillon, "Catholic Bishops Take Steps To Enforce Policy on Abuse," *The New York Times,* June 18, 2002, A19

8 Rachel Zoll, "Vatican approves sex-abuse policy," *The Star Ledger,* December 17, 2002, 6

9 *Lumen Gentium,* 4:37

10 Carol Eisenberg, "A New Cardinal Plan Stops short of 'zero tolerance'," *Newsday,* April 25, 2002, 1

11 Francis X. Clines, "Nearly 100 Kentucky Men Add to Accusations Against Priests," *The New York Times,* May 28, 2002

12 Pam Belluck, "Maine Parish Agonizes over a Priest's Confession," *The New York Times,* March 5, 2002, A1, 20

13 ibid.

14 Fox Butterfield, "Two Priests Who Abused Boys in Maine Are Removed," *The New York Times,* March 10, 2002, 33

15 Laurie Goodstein, "Accused of Sexual Assault, Archbishop Seeks to Retire," *The New York Times,* May 24, 2002, A1

16 ibid.

17 John W. Fountain, "Revelation About Payment Leaves Catholics Uneasy," *The New York Times,* May 25, 2002, A12

18 http://www.dallasnews.com/cgi-bin/2002/priests.cgi

[19] Peter Steinfels, "Beliefs; Crucial data is still needed to understand the extent of sexual abuse in the Catholic Church," *The New York Times,* May 4, 2002, B7

[20] ibid.

[21] Steve Adubato, Ph. D., "Church Leaders Must Do the Right Thing," www.politicsnj.com/adubato032802.htm

[22] William C. Symonds, "The Economic Strain on the Church," *Business Week,* April 15, 2002, 35

[23] ibid.

[24] Marie Szaniszlo, "I am 'sorry' –Contrite Law unveils pedophile priest policy," *The Boston Herald,* January 10, 2002, 1

[25] AP, "Fla. Bishop Admits to Abuse," March 8, 2002, CBSNEWS.com/stories/2002/03/08national/main.503337.shtml

[26] Theo Emery, "Lawyers to question Law and 3 bishops, Boston church leaders to discuss abuse cases," *The Star Ledger,* June 2, 2002, 15

[27] Nancy Phillips, "Lawsuit alleging abuse by priest is dismissed," *The Philadelphia Inquirer,* May 4, 2002, www.philly.com/mld/inquirer/living/religion/3196393.htm

[28] Brian T. Murray, "100 gather at Wayne church to discuss alleged abuse by Paterson Diocese priest," *The Star Ledger,* May 31, 2002, 26

[29] Rudy Larini and Brian T. Murray, "Bishop to repay diocese for abuse settlement," *The Star Ledger,* June 12, 2002, 1, 6

[30] AP, "Bishop Steps Down After Abuse Accusation," *The New York Times, May 23, 2002, A24*

[31] Laurie Goodstein, "Bishop Quits as Others Prepare to Meet on Abuse Scandal," *The New York Times,* June 12, 2002, A22

[32] Daniel J. Wakin, "Past Adviser to Cardinal O'Connor Resigns After Admitting to Affairs," *The New York Times,* June 12, 2002, B1

[33] James Sterngold, "Cardinal in Los Angeles Says He Let Abuser Remain a Priest," *The New York Times,* May 17, 2002, A19

[34] AP, "Report links abuse, priests and suicides, *The Star Ledger,* May 26, 2002, 17

[35] Daniel J. Wakin, "Priest Accused Of Sex Abuse Kills Himself, Authorities Say," *The New York Times, May 17, 2002, B1*

36 Erica Goode, "Study Finds Safety Problems At Center for Treating Clerics," *The New York Times,* May 25, 2002, A12

37 Pam Belluck, "Angry at Scandal, Lay Group Seeks Quiet Uprising in Pews," *The New York Times,* May 31, 2002, 1

38 J. M. Hirsch, "Petition Calls for McCormack's Resignation, *The Citizen Online,* May 1, 2002, fosters.com/citizen/news2002/ap0501aa.htm

39 Archbishop John. J. Myers, Homily, Chrism Mass, March 25, 2002, Cathedral Basilica of the Sacred Heart, http://www.rcan.org/archbish/jjm_homilies/jjmhomilies.htm

40 Angie Cannon; Katy Kelly; Nancy Bentrup, "Is There Any End in Sight?" *U.S. News & World Report,* April 22, 2002, 48

41 "Church Knew of Priest's Actions," *Los Angeles Times, April 9, 2002, www.Newsday.com*

42 ibid.

43 ibid.

44 ibid.

45 ibid.

46 Nancy Phillips

47 Laurie Goodstein, "California Dioceses Brace for New Abuse Suits as Law Allows Litigation of Old Cases," *The New York Times,* December 6, 2002, A28

48 ibid.

49 Sam Dillon and Leslie Wayne, "As Lawsuits Spread, Church Faces Questions on Finances," *The New York Times, June 13, 2002, 1, A36*

50 Pam Belluck, "A Plea for Understanding, and Money," *The New York Times,* May 6, 2002, A16

51 Pam Belluck, "Boston Church Panel Will Allow Archdiocese to Weigh Bankruptcy," *The New York Times,* December 5, 2002, 1

52 ibid.

53 ibid.

54 ibid.

55 Pam Belluck, "Judge Denies Church's Bid To Seal Records on Priests," *The New York Times,* November 26, 2002, A18

56 Editorial, "The Church and Chapter 11," *The New York Times,* December 5, 2002, A42

[57] Ken Maguire, "Files on Boston priests tell of sex and drugs with minors," *The Star Ledger,* December 4, 2002, 6

[58] ibid.

[59] ibid.

[60] Pam Belluck and Adam Liptak, "For Boston Archdiocese, Bankruptcy Would Have Drawbacks," *The New York Times,* December 3, 2002, A28

[61] ibid.

[62] ibid.

[63] Pam Belluck with Frank Bruni, "Law, Citing Abuse Scandal, Quits as Boston Archbishop and Asks for Forgiveness, A Yearlong Crisis, John Paul Accepts Move – Many Voice Relief over Resignation," *The New York Times,"* December 14, 2002, 1, A20

[64] Karen Freifield, "Priest admits to sexual abuse in unsigned '91 letter," *Newsday,* April 22, 2002, p1

[65] ibid.

[66] ibid.

[67] Meredith Gold, "Effects of sex abuse long-lasting, say experts," *Blethen Maine Newspapers, Inc.,* March 18, 2000, http://www.survivorsnetwork.org/

[68] Russ Olivo, "Healing Takes Time for Victims of Abuse," *The Woonsocket Call,* February 10, 2002, http://www.survivorsnetwork.org/

[69] David Crary, "For victims of abuse by clergy, the common bond is feeling of broken trust," AP, February 23, 2002, http://www.survivorsnetwork.org/

[70] ibid.

[71] Richard Nangle, "New circles of tragedy follow abuse," *Worcester Telegram & Gazette,* March 10, 2002, http://www.survivorsnetwork.org/

[72] Scott Shane and Del Quentin Wilber, "Sex abuse scandal profoundly personal," *Baltimore Sun,* May 15, 2002, http://www.survivorsnetwork.org/

[73] ibid.

[74] Jason Blair, "Man Who Shot Priest in an Abuse Case Wins Acquittal," *The New York Times,* December 17, 2002

75 Carl M. Cannon, "How Old News Became a National Story and Why It Took So Long," The Priest Scandal, 2002, http://www.survivorsnetwork.org/. The Doyle, Mouton, Peterson report was written in 1985. A 92-page confidential document, it outlined the problem of sex abuse by Catholic priests and recommended adoption of a national policy. Thomas P. Doyle is a priest and was then an advisor to the bishops. Rev. Michael Peterson was president of St. Luke Institute and F. Roy Mouton was an attorney familiar with the Gauthe case. Cf., Dawn Fallik, "1985 report cited increasing problem of sexual abuse," March 10, 2002, *Post Dispatch*, Stltoday.com

76 David Clohessy, "Impact Statement," USCCB, June 13, 2002

77 Scott Appleby, "The Church at Risk," Remarks to the USCCB, June 13, 2002

78 cf., Eileen Flynn and Gloria Thomas, *Living Faith*, Kansas City: Sheed & Ward, 1989. On pages 344-345 I describe how dualism and Jansenism detrimentally impact Catholic teaching about sex, undermining the belief that sex is an important part of God's good creation.

79 Eileen P. Flynn, "Honesty, openness is the way for Catholic church to recover," *Asbury Park Press*, April 26, 2002, A23

80 The Catechism of the Catholic Church was released in 1994 by the Vatican. Its purpose is to present the official Catholic teaching on faith and morals.

81 Flynn, "Honesty"

82 Covered mostly in regional newspapers and described in detail by Jason Berry in his benchmark book *Lead Us Not into Temptation*, NY: Doubleday, 1992.

83 James Porter abused children in five states. His misdeeds are chronicled in Philip Jenkins, *Pedophiles and Priests*, NY: Oxford University Press, 1996.

84 Edward Pipala molested dozens of boys while serving as a priest in the Archdiocese of New York; an account of his misconduct is contained in Jenkins.

85 The diocese of Dallas faced possible bankruptcy when victims of Rudolf Kos were awarded $119 million dollars. The amount of the settlement was later reduced to $30 million.

86 Sonia C. Solomonson, "I could die or heal," *The Lutheran*, June, 2002, 13

[87] Adam Liptak, "Religion and the Law," *The New York Times,* April 14, 2002, 1:30

[88] Laurie Goodstein and Sam Dillon, "Bishops Set Policy to Remove Priests in Sex Abuse Cases," *The New York Times,* June 15, 2002, A1, A13

[89] Rebecca Winters, "Catholicism in Crisis," *Time,* www.time.com

[90] Laurie Goodstein, "Abuse Victims Lay Blame at Feet of Catholic Bishops," *The New York Times,* June 14, 2002. A1, 33

[91] Pam Belluck, "Records Show Accused Priest Remained in Ministry," *The New York Times,* June 5, 2002, A21

[92] Appleby, 4

[93] John Tagliabue, "Are American Catholics Roman?" *The New York Times,* June 16, 2002, 4:1, 4:5

[94] Charles Krauthammer, "Church pulling its punches on crime," *The Star Ledger,* June 7, 2002, 41

[95] Charter, 4

[96] Richard Mc Brien, *Catholicism,* Minneapolis, MN: Winston Press, 1981, 799

[97] Raymond A. Schroth, "Untrue Contrition," *The Star Ledger,* June 19, 2002, 15

[98] Cf., Eileen P. Flynn, *Catholicism: Agenda for Renewal,* Lanham, MD: University Press of America, 1994. In this book I treat clericalism, juridicism and triumphalism at length and I reiterate my thinking in the remainder of this section.

[99] McBrien, p. 803

[100] John Paul II, *Ordinatio Sacerdotalis,* May 22, 1994

[101] Flynn, "Honesty"

[102] "Excerpt From Recommendation by Bishops' Committee on Sexual Abuse," *The New York Times,* June 5, 2002, A20

[103] Cozzens, 99

[104] Stephen J. Rossett, "The Catholic Church and Child Sexual Abuse," *America,* April 22, 2002, 11

[105] Press Release, "Gay Catholics Condemn Remarks by US Catholic Bishop and Conference President," April 23, 2002, www.dignityusa.org/news/020423-rome.html

[106] Cozzens, 132

[107] Jenkins, 92

[108] McBrien, 823

[109] *Lumen Gentium,* 33
[110] Catechism, 901
[111] 902
[112] 907
[113] 911
[114] Voice of the Faithful, www.voiceofthefaithful.org
[115] Catechism, 911
[116] Wilton D. Gregory, "Statement by President of the U.S. Catholic Bishops on Sexual Abuse," *The New York Times,* June 14, 2002, A32
[117] M. Steinfels, 2
[118] United States Conference of Catholic Bishops, "Essential Norms for Diocesan/Eparchial Policies Dealing with Allegations of Sexual Abuse of Minors by Priests or Deacons," June 14, 2002-October 29, 2002, 6
[119] 8A
[120] Laurie Goodstein, "Bishops Pass Plan To Form Tribunals In Sex Abuse Cases," *The New York Times,* November 14, 2002, 1, A30
[121] "Essential Norms," 6
[122] Goodstein, November 14, 2002
[123] Laurie Goodstein and Sam Dillon, "Meeting With Bishops, Victims Seek Strict Rules on Abuse," *The New York Times,* June 13, 2002, A37
[124] Cozzens, 113-114
[125] Appleby
[126] Cozzens, 116
[127] Symonds, 38-39
[128] Sam Dillon, "Bishops Fail to Heed Calls for an Audit," *The New York Times,* November 14, 2000, A30
[129] ibid.
[130] ibid.
[131] Sam Dillon, "Abuse Scandal Is Deterring Catholic Donors, Poll Says," *The New York Times,* November 9, 2002, A14
[132] Rossetti, 11-12
[133] Berry, 151
[134] Adam Liptak, "Abuse Victims Sue to Void Secrecy Provisions of Settlements With Church," *The New York Times,* June 7, 2002, A14
[135] Sam Dillon, "Abuse Victims Push to Talk With Bishops," *The New York Times,* June 10, 2002, p. A22.

136 Michael Paulson, "Grim audience hears accounts of abuse, call for reform," *The Boston Globe*, June 14, 2002, Boston.com

137 Thomas Farragher, "Globe is denied access as punishment for story," *The Boston Globe*, June 14, 2002, A40

138 Michael Paulson and Michael Rezendes, "Bishop Raps Critic of Abuse Policy," *The Boston Globe*, November 12, 2002, Boston.com

139 ibid.

140 Laurie Goodstein, "Catholic Bishops Seek to Reclaim Authority," *The New York Times*, November 12, 2002, A20

141 David Gibson, "Archbishop in Newark bans group," *The Star Ledger*, October 11, 2002, 1, 12

142 ibid.

143 Pam Belluck, "Cardinal Law Meets Leaders Of Lay Group," *The New York Times*, November 27, 2002, 1, A18

144 Gibson, 12

145 Daniel J. Wakin, "Priests Seek to Assert Rights and Fight Church Abuse Policy," *The New York Times*, October 4, 2002, B1

146 ibid.

147 ibid.

148 ibid.

149 Sam Dillon, "Catholic Religious Orders Let Abusive Priests Stay," *The New York Times*, August 10, 2002, A8

150 Laurie Goodstein and Sam Dillon, "Meeting with Bishops, Victims Seek Strict Rules on Abuse," *The New York Times*, June 13, 2002, A37

151 ibid.

152 Frank Keating, "Trying to Restore a Faith," *The New York Times*, June 15, 2002, A17

153 Laurie Goodstein, "Bishops Select Lay Board On Sexual Abuse Review," *The New York Times*, July 25, 2002, A10

154 ibid.

155 Anthony DePalma and Laurie Goodstein, "Member of Sex Abuse Panel Upsets Some," *The New York Times*, July 26, 2002, A16

156 Belluck, "Official Tells"

157 Michael Paulson, "Keating questions banning of lay group," October 5, 2002, Boston.com

[158] Laurie Goodstein, "Bishops Pick F.B.I. Official To Police Abuse in Church," *The New York Times,* November 8, 2002, A18

[159] ibid.

[160] ibid.

Printed in the United States
25194LVS00001B/430